Bolsena
Everything You Need to Know

Fleur Kinson

Published in April, 2004
by Norzia Press
130 Goosemoor Lane
Erdington, Birmingham (U.K.)
www.norziapress.co.uk

A catalogue record for this book is available from the British Library

ISBN 0-9547594-0-0

Cover photography by Fleur Kinson, Tom Lait (front bottom row left and
right), John McDermott (front green garden, and back red boat), and
Nicola Ker (back cyclist).
Cover design by Fleur Kinson.

Printed and bound by Quorum Technical Services Ltd., Cheltenham

To Dad and Mom

PLACE

PERSPECTIVE

PRACTICALITY

EMERGENCIES

EXPLORATION

ACKNOWLEDGEMENTS

My thanks must be given, above all, to **Bryn James**, for his heroic support and his unwavering belief in this project. His detailed textual comments, meanwhile, were invaluable (as always).

I would also like to thank:
Rachel Standring, who never runs out of ideas and who said "Why don't you write a book?" as we sat at the Café del Moro.
Dr. Penny Goodman, old friend from Oxford and fellow Brummie, who provided a well-polished window on the Roman world whenever I needed a clearer view.
Brad Sabin Hill, even older friend from Oxford and bibliophile extraordinaire, who provided a sanctuary when my stamina was waning.
Sue Hunting, for sending a useful book and offering a writer's empathy.
Guiliana Zucconi, for some insider gossip and good scholarship.
Ben Bath, for revealing certain 'Misteries'.
Sophia Warner, for creating a studious atmosphere in the first few days.
Christopher Whinney and ATG Oxford, for pointing me towards Bolsena in the first place.

This book was written between September 2003 and March 2004 in Bolsena, Taynton (Gloucestershire), Birmingham and Oxford.

PLACE

A Town, a Lake, a Secret World

Throughout their work on Lake Bolsena and its capital, physical geography and human history were judicious craftsmen – knowing exactly when to be flamboyantly creative and when to stand back and not interfere. After ferocious volcanic activity, physical geography left us the cleanest lake in Europe – teeming with fish, ringed by lushly fertile slopes, and basking in its own benign microclimate. It also did its work just where human history would enhance the place then completely fail to spoil it. Etruscans and Romans left their haunting traces, medieval and Renaissance builders provided palaces and cobbled piazzas, but moderners never covered the hillsides with featureless homes or clogged the tiny roads with traffic. Tourists, lured by their thousands into nearby Tuscany and Umbria, would overlook this precious corner of Lazio altogether; by the time they arrived in any significant number, so had ultra-modern ideas on sustainable tourism and sensitive development. Thus the loveliness of the giant crater part-filled by Lake Bolsena is assured – for now and for the foreseeable future. After many millennia in the making, the place has deftly been brought to perfection.

Pristine and uncrowded, this huge green-sided bowl with its glittering blue floor forms a private, almost secret little world. What lies beyond the crater is not only invisible from the inside, but holds less and less fascination to visitors mesmerized by the tranquility here. It is an arena in which newcomers quickly feel at home, a place which compels the same holidaymakers to return year after year.

The brightest jewel in this happy recess is Bolsena itself. Its 23 centuries of existence have culminated in a town of palpable contentment – well-maintained, litterless, crime-free. For the benefit of just 4,000 inhabitants, a fairytale castle rises above a tangle of medieval lanes, proud Renaissance homes gaze at each other across friendly squares, tree-lined boulevards lead down to clean beaches, and Roman ruins watch silently from the hillside above.

Living amidst such space and bounty has the Bolsenese suspecting the universe to be, at bottom, a kind and generous place. It explains why they are an unfailingly warm, guileless people. As visitors to Bolsena tend to be the peaceable sort who don't impoverish the town's atmosphere while they boost its finances, locals have never felt the need to dim the full, glaring beam of their native hospitality. They feel they've been born lucky in being born in this place. You love their town and want to spend time here? That just tells them you've got good sense.

Top Five Things to See and Do in Bolsena

(or This Book Distilled)

For demanding visitors with very little time. Also for unhurried visitors who want to combine minimum sightseeing with maximum sunbathing.

1. Explore the network of atmospheric medieval lanes.
2. Take a boat trip out to Bisentina Island (see <u>Bisentina Island</u>).
3. Visit the ruins of Roman Volsinii (see <u>Roman Volsinii and its Ruins</u>)
4. Visit the catacombs beneath Santa Cristina's Church (see <u>The Catacombs</u>)
5. Take my <u>Reed Tunnels and Black Beaches</u> walk (no. 2 in RECOMMENDED WALKS).

The Lake vs. the Sea

The charms of Bolsena aside, why go to Lake Bolsena when the Mediterranean is only thirty miles away? Because the lake and its shores are cleaner, better-looking, and more interesting than anything the local coastline has to offer. As a lifelong, hardcore devotee of the Mediterranean, it shocks me to say this. How could any land touching that most sacred sea be other than irresistible? The truth is that for a stretch of at least a hundred miles, the Tuscany-Lazio coast is characterless and scruffy – a series of undistinguished towns and modern developments flanking long but unremarkable beaches. Lake Bolsena, on the other hand, is charming – whichever way you look at it. And when you do look at it, there's so much *more to see*.

An ideal size and shape, you can usually see all the land surrounding the lake from any point along the shore; the water doesn't just wander off into the horizon. You can never view such entirety of the sea, of rivers, or even of long thin lakes. With its vision of contained enormity, Lake Bolsena encourages you always to look into the interesting distance. Gazers across the sea soon discover they can only look for so long at a flat line. And views across the lake are ever-changing. How much detail you see of the other side completely depends on the amount of moisture in the air. In dry, windy weather it's as if the opposite shore has leapt halfway across the water toward you, it's so unusually vivid. And because the lake lies in a crater, time of day determines which surrounding towns and lumps of land are best illuminated. Grotte di Castro, for example, was wholly invisible to me until I happened to look in the right direction at the right time of day. Had this town of several thousand people really always been there?

The lake simply has a greater diversity of faces than the sea, and it rotates them more frequently. A local once darkly confided to me, "The lake has moods." At the time I thought she'd been in the sun too long, but I think I've come to see what she meant. On a clear day, the early morning water-surface is a fantasy of different pale blues, the gauzy bedclothes of a lake still asleep and dreaming. You drive past slowly so as not to wake it. By noon it's a bowl of confident cobalt blue, far brighter than the sky and painful to look at. On a still, hazy day, a wide pool of mercury lies poised and perfectly flat before you. It'll turn to a rippled sheet of pewter, glinting and glowering, on a day of mixed sun and dark cloud. And you'll find yourself confronting a ferocious little ocean when the wind is high – the blue water churned to forbidding grey-brown and the waves smacking the beaches with astonishing savagery. Only rarely does the sky upstage the water – as it did in 2002 when the black funnel of a tornado dropped halfway down from clouds over the lake (see the photo of it in Il Gabbiano restaurant).

The sea might have its own range of moods, and it has some dramatic ones, but does it ever lie flat on its back dreaming or stretch motionless as a mirror? There is drama too, in extremes of stasis. While the lake can easily drop into a trance, the sea never rests – and it never fully stills its whispering tongue. The lake quite simply has a wider emotional vocabulary.

If you really must see the sea while you're near Lake Bolsena, take my advice and inch out from the mainland onto the Monte Argentario peninsula, or set sail for the islands of Elba or Giglio. All three represent the best seaside available for miles. But don't be surprised if you find yourself missing the lake and its ceaseless, beguiling variety.

The Cleanest Lake in Europe

Although you probably wouldn't fancy doing it near the petrol trails round the ports, Lake Bolsena is so clean you can drink it. Local fishermen go one better and *eat* it – a traditional fish and vegetable soup called *sbroscia* uses lakewater as its base. These two facts nearly became the stuff of history in the 1970s and 80s, when burgeoning tourist activity and local carelessness made the water unpalatable. You could tell just by looking that things weren't right. One Hydrobiological Institute able to record an amazing 15 metres of underwater visibility in 1965 could see for only 5 metres a decade later. Bolsena's authorities had been short-sighted – and were making others so. So they cleaned up their act, and these days the lake is drinkable once again. If you can't resist taking a quick sip, feel free.

A combination of geographical and historical factors allow Lake Bolsena to be Europe's cleanest. As it lies in a complex volcanic crater, dirty streams and rivers aren't what feed this lake but springs of very pure water which surface in fissures down on the lakebed. (Most emerge cold, but at least one runs at 40°C.) The lakefloor remains remarkably free of mud and organic matter, coated instead in fine volcanic sand. Of course, a squeaky clean set-up like this would be no match for polluting man, but no heavy industries have ever been established in the sparsely-populated area round the lake and so no nasty run-off has ever made it down the slopes into the water.

Wisely seeing a unique selling point in their lake's clarity, the authorities of all the surrounding towns have bent over backwards in recent years to protect it. No pollution from farms, homes or businesses is ever allowed to reach the precious blue. Underground around the lake's perimeter, a mighty circular collector discreetly gathers all the waste water and sewage generated locally and whisks it far away to be purified. Rest assured that this is one *very* clean lake. And don't worry for a nanosecond if you accidentally swallow a bellyful while swimming!

The Lake's Vital Statistics

perimeter: 43km
average distance across: 14km
surface area: 114km^2
maximum depth: 151m
average depth: 81m
volume of water: 9km^3
water level's height above sea level: 300m
position in size ranking of Italy's lakes: 5th largest
position in size ranking of Europe's volcanic lakes: 1st largest
total population of surrounding towns: roughly 20,000

PERSPECTIVE

[Note on PERSPECTIVE: So that these sections concerning history can be read separately or at random, it has very occasionally been necessary briefly to mention certain facts already discussed in previous sections. I hope chronological readers won't be troubled by this.]

Volcanic Activity

It's thrilling to imagine a volcano blowing itself to smithereens with such force it leaves a 270 km^2 hole in the landscape. When you gaze across Lake Bolsena and the land rising from its shores, everything you see is part of this crater. Imagine a volcano big enough to sit astride all that. Unfortunately for the imagination, this single cataclysmic eruption never happened. Contrary to what's implied by most texts which mention the lake, it wasn't one volcano but dozens of separate volcanoes and volcanic events taking place over many millennia which left us the huge basin now part-filled by Lake Bolsena.

Just under a million years ago, the area round the lake was a maze of volcanic cones and craters, lava spurting constantly through myriad fissures in volatile rock. This continual activity was nothing compared to the area's eruptive heyday, roughly 500,000 years ago, when extremely violent explosions steadily threw out enough subterranean material to empty the ground beneath the volcanoes. With a deafening whump, the resulting underground hollow eventually collapsed, creating a single vast crater – or 'volcanic-tectonic depression' if you want to be technical. Rain and springwater slowly eroded and expanded the giant new hole in the landscape and the lake began to take shape.

Having given birth to the lake, volcanic activity calmed down considerably for the next 380,000 years (perhaps content with what it had spawned). Then, final eruptions from two rogue volcanoes created the lake's islands: Martana and Bisentina, both being a hardened central 'plug' of ejected material. Once the burgeoning lake had been enhanced with these isles, all the local volcanoes promptly died. Slow erosive processes then modelled the land more pleasingly, plants grew, and animals and human beings eventually moved in on the area.

The volcanoes might all be dead, but their old stamping ground remains unstable. Tiny earthquakes imperceptible to all but specialist equipment flicker frequently through the area. Only very, very rarely do they more than flicker. Quakes hitting 5 on the Richter scale ravaged Bagnoregio in 1695 (seven miles from Bolsena as the crow flies), Gradoli in 1882 (eight miles away) and Tuscania in 1971 (21 miles away). But three serious seismic events in three hundred years is not a bad track record, and you should sleep very soundly in your bed while in Bolsena.

As a legacy of its volcanic origins, the lakefloor still sees some emanations of gas and hot springwater, but nothing you'll be able to observe unless you don specialist equipment and go down there. Stretches of black sand on the shore more readily recall the lake's explosive past, preserving the story in a million tiny filaments of black, green and colourless glass. Walkers enjoying my Reed Tunnels and Black Beaches route will see the best of this glittering sand, and also encounter the *'Pietre Lanciate'* ('thrown stones') where ancient lava cooling at different rates created an impressive rockface of sprouting prisms – a sideslung version of Ireland's Giant's Causeway.

Who Was Here First?

At least 30,000 years ago, before he was wiped out by the rather more cunning *Homo sapiens sapiens*, the early hominid *Homo sapiens neanderthalensis* was in the Lake Bolsena area, busily making flaked stone tools to inform later archaeologists of his presence. 7,000-year-old artefacts suggesting domestic life have been dug out of the hills just south of Bolsena, and it's generally agreed that human settlement round the lakeshore has been continuous for the last 5,000 years or so. Given the immensely fertile land, the mild climate, rich supply of fish, ready access to clean water and so on, none of this should surprise us. Some of the early settlements appear to have been sizeable. The bones, pottery and wooden stakes of a 3,000-year-old 'Villanovan' city (the dominant civilization in these parts before the rise of Etruscan culture) were hauled out from beneath the water a few decades ago. The city seems to have existed for at least a couple of centuries.

Like Italy's other volcanic lakes, the water of Lake Bolsena has risen for the last three millennia (although the level seems to have stabilized now, and you shouldn't fear that the crater is going to keep filling up like a bathtub till it overflows). The rising water has allowed us to learn far more about Bronze and Iron Age settlements concealed by the waves than about those which were not. Underwater, oxygen can't eat into objects quite as devastatingly as it does on land, so historical artefacts – especially wooden ones – are preserved comparatively well. Scuba-clad archaeologists have done a great deal of work down on Bolsena's lakefloor. Indeed, many of the techniques of Underwater Archaeology – a relatively new academic discipline – were pioneered there.

Visitors interested in all these things should make a beeline to the Territorial Museum of Lake Bolsena housed inside the castle at the top of the town. The texts of the museum's explanatory panels were finally translated into English in 2003 and can be bought as a smart little book called *The Polyglot Museum*. While you're there, make sure you climb up the spiral staircase in the courtyard outside to catch an eagle's-eye-view of Bolsena and the lake. For current opening times, call the museum on 0761-798630.

Etruscans and Romans

For most of us, 'Etruscan' is one of those words we've met many times but, if pressed, couldn't precisely explain. We might know the word has a connection with Tuscany. We might even know that the Etruscans were a people, and that they did impressive things of some kind. But like 'Phoenicians' and 'Carthaginians', they tend to be just a name with no picture – another obscure, long-dead ethnic group only really familiar to people with a Classical education (and perhaps not all that familiar to them either).

I'm asking you to sharpen up your hazy understanding now because the Etruscans are the people who founded Bolsena. You should know who they were if you come here. (And anyway, you're going to meet that word 'Etruscan' *everywhere* you go for miles and miles in the area around Bolsena. Think of the irritation saved by clearing it up right here.) One thing though, it's a well-founded cliché that anyone who starts learning about the Etruscans quickly becomes hooked on the subject. If you can't bear to acquire a new interest, look away now.

For half a millennium or more, the Etruscans were Europe's most advanced civilization outside Greece. Made wealthy on international trade, they spent their time draining marshes, painting delicate vases, building a network of roads, making wine, fashioning exquisite jewellery, founding great cities, writing a body of literature, carving water tunnels through sheer rock, creating breathtaking sculptures, and erecting aqueducts. Hmmm, sounds a bit like the Romans, doesn't it? Well it should. Consider three facts: at least two of Rome's earliest kings were Etruscans; most Romans had some Etruscan ancestors; the Romans took many of their ideas on art, law, religion, public institutions, social customs, water management and road-building directly from the Etruscans. You owe far more to the Etruscans than you probably imagine. Even your living room walls might reflect their influence (see Tarquinia in the RECOMMENDED EXCURSIONS BY CAR).

So why haven't you heard more about these people? Because they were completely overshadowed by the Romans. And because so much of what they did was lost before historians could grasp it and imprint it on our popular map of the past. Building almost exclusively in wood, a material effortlessly consumed by centuries, the Etruscans left behind no temples, amphitheatres or triumphal arches (for example) to stamp their civilization onto our consciousness. They don't bring themselves to life by speaking from the page, either. While early Roman schoolboys studied Etruscan literature as part of their curriculum, modern-day scholars can barely understand a word of the language (it's not part of the Indo-European family, related instead to some similarly opaque and long-dead Mediterranean tongues). The Etruscans' most extensive written works, in which they describe their religious practices, were lost forever when Christian Roman Emperors eager to stamp out paganism burnt every volume to ashes. The Etruscans themselves seemed unconcerned with preserving their glory for posterity. When their civilization was subsumed into Roman civilization, they felt no compulsion to assert a self-consciously distinct ethnicity, and readily adopted Roman ways. With so little testament to the Etruscans' existence, and *so much* testament to the spectacular existence of the Romans, popular and academic attention has understandably always concentrated on the latter. Indeed, scholarship on things Etruscan only really got going at all in the last century or two – and what texts there are still brim with words like 'mysterious', 'unknown', and 'enigmatic'. Etruscan civilization might have been rescued from historical oblivion, but only just.

What *is* known is that the Etruscans lived across a large swathe of Italy encompassing modern-day Tuscany, western Umbria, and northern Lazio. Their civilization had its roots in what we now call 'Villanovan' culture, which existed across and beyond the same area from the 9th Century B.C. (and was distinguished by its funerary practices and so on). Wily Greeks, exploring western Italy for minerals in the 8th Century B.C., encountered these comparatively primitive Villanovans and began filling their heads with ideas. They traded with them, showed them various technologies, and taught them to write (this is how the Etruscan language came to be written in Greek letterforms. The evolved Etruscan alphabet was later snapped up by Latin-speakers and shaped into our enduring Roman alphabet).

Put simply, Greeks galvanized the Villanovans with whom they had contact – to such an extent that the people became something else. They became a recognizably new civilization worthy of a new name: the Etruscans. In Greek-style ships, these Etruscans were soon whisking raw materials across the Med to Greece, Sardinia, Spain and Egypt, and getting rich enough on the proceeds to support a great civilization – a civilization which would develop technological innovations of its own and whose political power would spread far beyond its native territory. The intimate relationship with Greece would weather the centuries, however, as is suggested by two stray facts: more Greek pottery has been found in Etruscan tombs than in Greece itself; and, in a coals-to-Newcastle coup, Etruscan potters eventually supplied Greece's domestic market with perfect Greek-style pots.

Fittingly, it was the Greeks who provided an enduring name for this new civilization. They called the people the *Tyrsenoi* or *Tyrrhenoi* – which later gave rise, via Latin, to words like 'Etruria', 'Tyrrhenian', 'Etruscan' and 'Tuscany'. The key element in these words is probably the ancient, linguistically-widespread word *tir* or *tur* meaning 'tower' or 'tall rocky hill' (which British readers might recognize in Glastonbury Tor). The Greeks and Romans seemed to think of the Etruscans as a tower-people, and indeed most of their settlements were in high places or made use of tall defensive structures. The Etruscans, by the way, called themselves the *Rasna* or *Rasenna* (perhaps giving the Greeks the 'rsen' in *Tyrsenoi*). Like *Cymru* to the Welsh, this native name might just mean 'the people'. Virgil meanwhile, being a poet and drawn to facts alcoholic, referred to them in his *Aeneid* as the '*Oenotri*' ('wine-makers').

Whatever the names given to them, they got on with being who they were from around the 8th Century B.C. until the advent of the Christian era. The beginning of the end came when a little town called Rome started to get ideas above its station. From the 4th Century B.C., Romans began a slow but systematic conquest of Etruria. Their policy wasn't slash and burn, but colonize and control. While many Etruscan cities resisted, others meekly allied themselves with the awesomely organized newcomers. The last Etruscan city to fall to Roman control was Velzna in 264 B.C., whence came the founders of Bolsena (see next section). The Romans were relatively benign masters to the Etruscans, charmed as they were by their achievements and recognizing that they could learn things from them. But this Roman respect wasn't enough to prevent the Etruscans' erasure. As is perhaps inevitable when one bunch of overachievers lives amongst another bunch of overachievers, the two civilizations became less and less distinct. In 89 B.C., all Etruscans were granted Roman citizenship. They had been turned into Romans - literally.

It can be useful to think of the Etruscans as occupying one rung on a grossly oversimplified genealogy of modern European civilization. Thus, the ancient Egyptians shot the spark of organized, creative life to the Minoans and others who passed it to the Greeks who shared it with the Etruscans who fuelled the Romans who spread a fire across the rest of Europe. The true evolution of European civilization is, of course, a bit more complicated. But the Etruscans certainly deserve a place among its most significant players.

Changing Places, Changing Names – Velzna to Volsinii to Bolsena

Lake Bolsena wasn't unknown to the Etruscans – nor to their forerunners, the Villanovans. These earlier people were enjoying life on the eastern shores of the lake in the 9th Century B.C., and they conveniently left us the now-underwater remains of a city to tell us so. By the 8th Century B.C., Villanovans having 'become' Etruscans, the lakeside saw its first significant Etruscan settlement: Vesentum or Bisentium. It sat on the curious domed hill now called Monte Bisenzio on the southern shore, and perhaps sprawled as far as modern-day Capodimonte. Objects of typical Etruscan sophistication have been unearthed from Monte Bisenzio, including sandals, false teeth, and a decorated cart made of bronze. But no settlement persists on the hill today. Unlike on the other side of the lake, where a later Etruscan town is still going strong. It's called Bolsena.

In 264 B.C., the Romans finally managed to defeat one of the greatest of Etruscan cities, Velzna – widely believed to have been situated at modern-day Orvieto, 15 miles northeast of Bolsena. Rather than kill everyone in the city (not the Romans' style), the conquerors rehoused all of Velzna's survivors on a certain empty hillside overlooking a beautiful blue lake. The relocation was intended as a pride-denting punishment for daring to fight against Roman control. Thus Bolsena's earliest incarnation was as a refugee camp or a Milton-Keynes-like contrived community, depending how you look at it. This brand new Etruscan town fondly held onto the name of the lost city, Velzna. But as the Romans controlled it (from a distance), its name was very often run through Roman mouths and Latin grammar, coming out as *Volsinii*. This Roman form persists today in the name of the Volsini hills which surround the lake.

Modern-day Bolsena is still called Velzna, of course. It's just that some of the sounds have been buckled by time. V turning into B – or vice versa – is a very common pronunciation change in European languages (consider sounds in the history of Greek and Spanish). It's only a tiny step for the top front teeth to slide off – or onto – the bottom lip. Z turning into S is even easier, as the mouth keeps the same position but ceases the effort of engaging the voicebox. Vowels, flighty things made only of air, have always blown hither and thither at the drop of a het. Thus it's easy to imagine a series of pronunciation shifts running Velzna to Volzna to Volzena to Volsena to Bolsena, or something similar, with Volsinii getting in there tangentially along the way.

That Bolsena began when Etruscans from the original Velzna were ejected by Romans in 264 B.C. is fairly certain. What's rather more in doubt is the original location of mighty Velzna. Was it really Orvieto? Or was it somewhere much nearer modern-day

Bolsena? And what of the empty hillside to which the Etruscans were banished? Had it really seen no prior Etruscan settlement and were the Velzna refugees its first inhabitants? What of the 4th Century B.C. walls found locally, engraved with Etruscan letters, and the remains of a temple already abandoned by the 3rd Century B.C.? For specialists on these topics, a certain amount of debate continues.

Roman Volsinii and its Ruins

For a century or so, the new Velzna or Volsinii maintained a distinctly Etruscan flavour and structure, despite nominally being controlled by Rome. A vast new road would change all that from the 150s B.C., putting Volsinii squarely on the main highway running north from Rome to the Alps. Inevitably, the Roman through-traffic integrated the town more and more intimately with the Roman world and Roman ways of doing things. You could say that the Via Cassia quite decisively transformed 'Velzna' into 'Volsinii'.

The Romanization of once-Etruscan Volsinii coincided, of course, with a general Romanization of much of Italy in the 1st Century B.C. Various Italian peoples labouring under the yoke of Rome let it be known around this time that they rather fancied a bit of parity with their Roman masters – votes, citizenship and the like. Incensed at such presumption, the Romans instigated a series of Social Wars against their subjects (a memorable oxymoron, war being distinctly antisocial). Romans won all these wars as a matter of course – and then decided to give the other Italians what they'd wanted in the first place. Volsinii's little Social War came in 89 B.C. When it was over, Volsinii was elevated to the status of Municipality and was absorbed completely into the Roman world.

As a thoroughly Roman town, Volsinii flourished. Noble families moved in, and the town became a holiday resort (even then!) for rich officials. The first four centuries of the Christian era were Volsinii's 'golden age', seeing the construction of an aqueduct, forum, theatre, amphitheatre, and numerous grand buildings with public inscriptions. The later part of this period saw a growing Christian community in the town – especially following the martyrdom of a young convert (see Local Hero section below). The cult which grew up around little Santa Cristina can be seen as another mutation in a long line of females revered in Bolsena. The original Etruscans sent from old Velzna were dippy about Northia or Norzia, their goddess of destiny. The Volsinii Romans diverted this attention to their own Fortuna, who similarly meted out fate and bounty, and kept soft spots too for Ceres, Minerva, and Venus.

Even this mini-pantheon of kindly goddesses, however, couldn't protect Volsinii forever. By the 4th Century A.D., the Roman Empire was collapsing. Rome itself (a backwater now the Empire's capitals had moved elsewhere) was sacked by Visigoths in 410. The same century saw the fall of Volsinii. Longobards swooped down and trashed the place, turning the once-proud Roman town into a field of ruins – ruins that would later serve as a stone quarry for the building of medieval Bolsena. Their town in tatters, the remaining community of Volsinii shifted itself to the little cliff where the castle now stands, and patiently waited out the Dark Ages.

Thanks to archaeological excavations undertaken by The French School at Rome, it's possible to spend an evocative hour or so wandering the ruins of Roman Volsinii today. Most of the ancient city's remains still lie submerged across the hillside, but about 100m from Bolsena's castle archaeologists have unearthed a forum, a ruined basilica, and two private houses adorned with delicate frescos and floors of mosaic and marble. See if you can spot some of the esoteric graffiti early Christians carved into the forum's paving stones in order to subversively signal their presence to each other. (There's a tiny palm branch, for example, touchingly immortal amidst living weeds).

The setting of the excavated site (*'Volsinii Scavi'*) is very picturesque, ringed by olive groves and punctuated with views of the lake's electric blue. It attracts surprisingly few visitors and has a tranquil atmosphere. Fallen columns are watched over by the timeless black silhouettes of cypress trees; capitals litter the scrub grass, pinecones nestling among them like admiring offspring. Entry to the site is free, and it's open till 1pm every day except Monday.

Half-Buried Treasure – the Mercatello Amphitheatre

In the sloping farmland immediately northeast of what has been excavated of Volsinii, several giant-cobblestoned Roman roads rattle off into the undergrowth in perfectly straight lines. These are long-forgotten streets of the ancient city, arranged in a grid and all oriented north-south or east-west. Lying in their midst are the remains of a Flavian-period amphitheatre. It would have gone up around the same time as the Colosseum, but unlike Rome's showpiece this site is almost wholly unexcavated and lies submerged by dirt and plant life. No well-worn paths or signs direct any attention to the amphitheatre, and most visitors to Bolsena never learn of its existence.

When you find it, the arena is plainly visible – a flat oval pan now covered with scrubby grass. The tiered seating, except for a stretch of exposed masonry on the western edge, is completely concealed beneath trees. Thus the bowl shape of the amphitheatre is perfectly retained, but rendered in vegetation. A casual peek under the skirt of branches soon reveals the dirt-submerged slope of seating, with bits of exposed stone poking through here and there. In spring and autumn, wild pink cyclamen grow quietly in the shade under these trees, precisely where spectators once sat.

I'm reliably informed that there were plans – and funding – to excavate the site. Work began, the western section was unearthed and its stones marked with little numbers (still visible). Then something went wrong. The funding was squandered (or withdrawn for some other reason) and work stopped. There are no plans for excavation work to start again. It might seem incredible, but a site like this has little academic value to archaeologists and Roman historians, who expect to learn nothing really new or revelatory from it. A full excavation would take about two to three years – a lot of time when you expect to learn very little. Certainly as far as tourism goes, a fully excavated amphitheatre would be a great attraction, but it would just be one more feather (and a costly one) in Bolsena's already well-festooned cap. So this secret bit of treasure is likely to remain hidden for a long time yet.

Actually, its state of neglect lends the amphitheatre a poignancy which careful excavation might diminish. Standing in the deserted grassy arena, you know that this utterly abandoned spot was once the focus of intense excitement, presented a climax to days which were then the peak of modernity. You imagine the relaxed, confident people of Volsinii enjoying a festive spectacle, not one of them thinking that in nearly two thousand years' time an occasional explorer might be wandering over the buried ruins of their venue marvelling at its antiquity and at the impossibly archaic lives of those who used it.

To reach the amphitheatre, you must follow the main road toward Orvieto which winds up and out of Bolsena. A car is best, but the route is not impossible for pedestrians (and they should ignore outdated maps which erroneously suggest possible shortcuts along country lanes). Go past the Volsinii excavations, following the road as it veers left, round a hairpin bend to the right, and along a short stretch where trees line both sides of the road. At the end of the trees, on the left, there is a nicely-paved little driveway flanked by stone pillars. Ignore it, and carry on a fraction further until you see on the left a pair of neglected grey metal gates in front of a grassy path. (Car drivers might like to park in the viewing area on the right a few seconds further on. Pedestrians, having walked this far, should perhaps treat themselves to the great view available here, too.) Walk around the grey gates and carry on up the faint path, through a meadow dotted with olive trees and alongside a rustic wooden fence. At the top right corner of the meadow, veer to the right where a path goes between trees, and you'll soon emerge onto the most exposed edge of the amphitheatre. (Note that the nearby Roman roads are not immediately accessible from the amphitheatre site. To see them, you have to crash around exploratively in farmland flanking the site – best reached by paths before and after the grey-gated one you came in on.)

Local Hero – Santa Cristina

Despite being only eleven or twelve, Cristina was a model of teenage rebellion – defying her parents' wishes, opting for an alternative lifestyle, and remaining stubbornly immune to all threats and persuasion. Her father Urbanus was a high-powered Roman official, the Prefect of Volsinii, elected by Emperor Diocletian himself. He was mortified when his daughter converted to the then new-fangled faith of Christianity and changed her own name to bring herself closer to Christ. It really didn't look good for a man of his standing in the pagan Roman world to harbour a religious subversive within his own family – *especially* when his employer was the most virulently anti-Christian of all Rome's Emperors. Urbanus's position demanded that he act. Entreaties turned to threats, threats to imprisonment and finally to attempted murder.

Unhindered by paternal love, Urbanus threw his daughter into the lake with a rock tied to her ankle. Miraculously, so the story goes, the rock floated back to shore with Cristina on board, her footprints marking the basalt as if it were wet cement. (This magic lump of stone is still on display in Santa Cristina's church, and indeed a pair of footprints are imprinted on it.) Horrified at his failure to drown his daughter, or consumed by guilt, Urbanus promptly died, leaving two subsequent Prefects to try to 'persuade' the headstrong child to give up Christ.

A real martyr's martyr, Cristina was prepared to take anything they threw at her. Indeed her relentless survival begins to remind one of Wile E. Coyote in a Road Runner cartoon. A composite list of her alleged tortures would be long and disturbing. Ancient sources vary, but there is usually talk of snakes, ovens, whips, the wheel and rack, a boiling cauldron and so on. It's likely that fevered early martyrologists made much of this stuff up or conflated it with the suffering of other saints (notably St. Christina of Tyre, who herself might have been fictional). But what's fairly certain is that in the end Cristina was shot through with arrows and killed – on July 24th of an unidentified year in the early 4th Century. Buried in the catacombs reserved for Volsinii's burgeoning Christian community, a cult soon grew up around her – as naturally it might around a murdered child.

Today the people of Bolsena keep alive the memory of their town's patron saint with the annual '*Misteri di Santa Cristina*' festival (the '*misteri*' alluded to here are 'mysteries' in the sense of 'divine revelations'). On the evening of 23rd July and throughout the following morning, silent and static scenes or *tableaux vivants* from Cristina's life are presented repeatedly on wooden stages erected round the town. Lavishly-costumed locals stand in dramatic poses depicting Cristina floating on her stone, being wrapped in snakes, being cooked in a cauldron, being shot with arrows, her father being carried to hell by devils, etc. – the Italian flair for all aspects of visual presentation very much in evidence! Curtains part to let you inspect each living picture for several minutes, then close again to give the actors a rest before the next showing. Meanwhile an image of Cristina is solemnly carried up through the town from her church to that of San Salvatore and back down again, pausing before each of the scenes so that the saint's brief life can flash in front of her eyes.

The Catacombs

Eerie and otherworldly, the catacombs where young Cristina rests are one of the most fascinating places in Bolsena and shouldn't be missed. Hundreds of horizontal niches for bodies, stacked vertically along branching corridors, have been carved underground into soft volcanic rock. The older tombs, from the 3rd Century, are those at the top – deeper digging having been done over the next hundred-plus years as more tombs were needed. With no straight lines in evidence, the place has the feel of a weird natural structure – like a giant, half-melted beehive. Some of the later, lower tombs remain sealed with mortar, traces of frescoed portraits and inscriptions still poignantly visible upon them. The low lighting and undisturbed air, combined with the bizarre Indiana Jones atmosphere of the place, can daze you a bit. If you're lucky enough to be down there alone, go to the very end of the central corridor and stand perfectly still. Except for the occasional distorted sound drifting in from the church, it is *completely* silent and you can hear only your own breathing and your ears squealing.

To visit the catacombs, buy an inexpensive entry ticket from the tiny bookshop inside Santa Cristina's Church. You will be let through some locked gates into Santa Cristina's Grotto and from here you can descend into the catacombs (and go across to the misleadingly-named 'Lombard Cemetery', another section of the catacombs). The site is visitable between 9am and 12 noon year-round, then from 4 to 6pm in summer and from 3 to 5:30pm in winter. To confirm details or opening times, contact the curator: 0761-799067.

The Slow Evolution of Santa Cristina's Church – I

Soon after her death, Cristina's local star status prompted the establishment of a cave-like little church next to the catacombs. It was carved into an adjoining rockface and served as her only shrine for more than six centuries. During that time, Cristina's fame spread far and wide, thanks to Bolsena's position on the great north-south artery (and Rome-pilgrimage route) of the Via Cassia. By the 5th Century, Christians throughout Western Europe and North Africa revered her. By the 9th Century, the whole European continent had joined in the chorus of her praise.

In the 1070s, it was decided that the young martyr deserved something grander than an old cave as her temple. Thus Pope Gregory VII and the Countess of Tuscany organized the construction of a fine new romanesque church several metres from the grotto-cum-shrine. It would give a better impression of the town to Rome-bound pilgrims stopping off in Bolsena to pay homage to its most famous daughter. The old grotto and the new church were to remain separate until a significant 13th Century event, described below, led eventually to their integration.

The new space available in which to praise her naturally increased Cristina's bankability. She had become such hot property by the 1100s that fistfuls of her bones were snatched by enterprising thieves and traded on the European relics black market. Only a little bit of Cristina's skeleton currently remains in her home town. The rest languishes in Palermo cathedral.

The Eucharist Miracle – a Gripping Tale of Blood and Magic

In 1263, a priest named Peter was travelling from his native Prague to Rome on a pilgrimage. He was worried sick about his faith, finding it impossible to believe that the body and blood of Christ manifested themselves in Eucharistic bread and wine. Like so many pilgrims travelling the Via Cassia, he stopped in Bolsena to celebrate mass. Ardently he prayed to Santa Cristina that she might persuade God to grant him new belief. As he held aloft a Eucharistic wafer and broke it for eating, blood sprang from it – enough blood to soak into the altarcloth and stain the white marble altarstones. You can imagine the commotion. (As could the painter Raphael, later depicting the scene in his *Mass at Bolsena* – on display in the Vatican Museums.)

It's safe to assume that Peter went back to Prague with a somewhat strengthened faith. Meanwhile, the blood-stained altarcloth was excitedly sent to Pope Urban IV, who happened to be in nearby Orvieto. Impressed, the pontiff proclaimed the incident a genuine Miracle and promptly ordered that a mighty cathedral be built in Orvieto to house such a holy bolt of cloth. (Thus Bolsena lost another of its sacred objects. While Orvieto gained one of Italy's most stunning buildings.) Excitement spreading, a papal bull was drawn up instigating the annual feast of Corpus Christi – which has been celebrated ever since throughout the Catholic world. The 'stained' altarcloth is still on display in Orvieto cathedral, while the discoloured altarstones remain in Bolsena, one permanently on show in the Miracle Chapel of Santa Cristina's Church.

(Hardcore rationalists might like to know that the starch-loving bacterium *Serratia marcescens* causes blood-red spots to bloom on bread contaminated with it. Spots to drops to running blood would constitute only a very modest expansion in a story that's been going for several centuries, and/or in the perception of original observers gripped by strong emotion. The staining of cloth and marble, of course, is an entirely different matter.)

The Infiorata

As you might imagine of an international Holy Day which was spawned on their doorstep, the feast of Corpus Christi is celebrated with particular gusto by the people of modern-day Bolsena. Under the early summer sun, the medieval streets are lined with a million flower petals fashioned into elaborate pictures and patterns. A procession then carries the town's sacred relics along the pretty carpet and transforms it to damp mush. Creating this vast mosaic of petals is an enormous enterprise. The effort involved, and the loveliness of the result, make the final trampling all the more poignant a sacrifice.

Almost the whole population of Bolsena spends the day on the streets, kneeling on the cobbles and tarmac sketching lines, hefting bags and boxes full of flower petals carefully separated into neat piles of individual colours, and patiently putting the soft fragments into place. By mid-afternoon, bright swathes of pictures are already visible around the feet of the happy labourers – huge ambitious portraits of Christ, biblical scenes, cherubs, intricate floral patterns painstakingly repeated over hundreds of yards. The secular observer might smile to note how lavish are the nude portraits of Eve, how erotic any scenes of her and Adam. Mary's lips are always ruby red. Even the cherubs are lascivious and ripe to the touch. Physical love, it seems, just cannot be frowned upon in frisky Italy, and flesh never anything but delighted in, even in a strongly religious context. Hearts are the universal ornament here. Love is really what is being celebrated – divine *and* earthly.

As the artwork nears completion, coach after coach of tourists and residents of nearby towns arrive, slowly filling Bolsena to the brim. Various excitements get underway in Piazza Matteotti, such as young men in medieval costumes twirling and tossing giant flags to a background of drums and trumpets. As 6 o'clock nears, the Bolsenese work in an escalating, ecstatic panic down on the cobbled lanes while a mass of visitors squeezes sweatily past, gasping and angling cameras.

And then at 6, with the very last petal thrust into place, solemn chaos begins up in Piazza Santa Cristina. Worthies in ragged-edged groups teem out of Santa Cristina's Church into a thickly assembled crowd and try to commence the procession. No one takes charge, no one quite knows what's going on, and there's a lot of stopping and starting. A clutch of priests gaze round in their sunglasses for guidance. Pious matrons with lace headgear inch hesitantly forward in short skirts and steep heels. A gigantic wooden cross sways worryingly above colourful banners embroidered with the crests of local towns. Then everything lurches forward as band members in dazzling uniforms start a fumbling tune.

For two hours the dense, messy parade shuffles round the town, churning flower petal pictures into abstracts underfoot. On the main Via Cassia, traffic waits bewildered and hot for the palaver to pass. Near the castle, there are cartoon-like scenes as the whole procession squeezes farcically in and out of metre-wide alleyways. After an excess of public praying outside the church of San Salvatore, where the relics will spend the night, everyone weaves back through town to Santa Cristina's Church.

If all this sounds a jolly wheeze to you and you'd like to ensure your visit to Bolsena coincides with Corpus Christi Day (called

'Corpus Domini' in Italy), you'll have to arrange it with a table of moveable feasts to hand. The festival usually falls in late May or early June.

The Slow Evolution of Santa Cristina's Church – II

With a prestigious miracle *and* a widely-revered saint on its CV, Bolsena's religious importance swelled considerably throughout the Middle Ages. The little palaeo-Christian church-in-the-rock and its romanesque companion swelled too, reflecting the town's significance. They would go on sprouting annexes and attachments for several centuries until they became the unified cluster of buildings we see today. Whether you find the present-day Church a discordant hotchpotch of architecture or a bold harmony of diverse building styles, you cannot deny that it's a memorable pile of stone.

If you're standing in front of the collection of buildings, facing them, the smooth-browed little unit on the right is the 15th Century oratory of St. Leonard – now the sacristy. Moving left, there is the 'major church' with its frontage of basic geometric shapes. Built in 1078 with a nave and two aisles, this romanesque building has been altered repeatedly (most recently in the 1920s when the interior was comprehensively restored). The elegant facade was added in the 1490s, at the request of Cardinal Giovanni de' Medici and the people of Bolsena. Its distinctly Florentine look is no accident. The Florentine sculptor brothers who worked on it, Benedetto and Francesco Buglioni, probably adapted a design they had put in for the design competition for Florence Cathedral's facade. The surface decoration is particularly attractive. Note the numerous appearances of 'the Green Man'. (He can also be seen on the medieval marble archway connecting the major church's interior to that of the Miracle Chapel – along with other exotica like a basilisk and a chimera).

The obligatory – and lovely – campanile was commissioned in the late 13th Century by Cardinal Ranieri. In my opinion it's vital to the cohesion of the building(s), drawing the eye up and creating the illusion of a triangle rather than a horizontal *line* which could much more easily appear to break into separate bits. (It's the same trick artistic gardeners use with carefully-placed tall plants, giving lower-level growth a sense of unity by making it seem part of a larger triangle – the brain imagines the lower stuff 'leaning' towards the high point and fills in the gaps.) If you don't believe me, try imagining the whole Church without the campanile. Dull, isn't it? And the buildings suddenly seem much more separate.

The much-maligned 'yellow oval bit' topped with a cupola helps significantly in bolstering the imaginary scalene triangle. It is the upper part of the Miracle Chapel, built in 1693 to house the holy altarstones stained by the bleeding Eucharist bread exactly four hundred years earlier. (The unprepossessing facade went up in 1863.) The construction of this Miracle Chapel finally linked the rest of the Church to its oldest part – the 'minor church' or original temple, half dug into the rockface above the catacombs. Inside, passing through a large 16th Century openwork screen, you meet the *c*.8th Century altar where the Eucharist miracle took place, fronted by Cristina's miraculous floating millstone complete with footprints. Beyond them lies the saint's main shrine with 19th Century railings and staircases, plus a superb Benedetto Buglioni terracotta of recumbent Cristina looking supremely at peace. The overhead frescos here are 16th Century, while the watchful St. Peter is 15th Century. You can descend to Cristina's simple 4th Century sarcophagus (note the damage done by medieval bone-thieves), and go on into the catacombs.

Medieval and Renaissance Bolsena

As Santa Cristina's Church expanded over the centuries, so of course did the rest of Bolsena. A medieval building frenzy saw the erection of the old walled town with its cobbled lanes and gated archways, plus the construction of the earliest bit of the castle or *rocca* (ordered by Pope Hadrian IV in 1156). The castle's largest tower went up in the late 1200s, but the whole structure only started to look like a 'proper' castle when the Monaldeschi della Cervara family built the other towers a century later to keep the first one company. Meanwhile, beyond the snug walls of the little town, *another* castle had gone up near Santa Cristina's Church, and dwellings had been built around it. So medieval Bolsena was really *two* little towns – the '*borgo dentro*' (town inside the walls) and the '*borgo fuori*' (town outside the walls) – each watched over by its own castle. The rival castle was razed to the ground – along with much of the *borgo fuori* – in the late 1300s when papal mercenaries from Brittany ran riot in Bolsena. Incidentally, earlier that century Bolsena had allegedly been spared destruction when the women of the town chanted a thousand '*Ave Maria*'s and miraculously repelled a would-be siege by King Ludwig IV of Bavaria. (He probably just got a headache and lost interest.)

During the Renaissance, Bolsena's fame and importance decreased markedly. But it remained the favourite holiday destination of politico-religious heavyweights like Giovanni de' Medici (later made Pope Leo X), Cardinal Tiberio Crispo, and Popes Pius II and Paul III. (Bolsena has never stopped seducing visitors, you see.) Medici did all sorts of commendable things in Bolsena like reorganizing civil government, arranging a pretty Florentine facade for Santa Cristina's Church, having a public fountain built in Piazza San Rocco, and so on. Crispo, meanwhile, busied himself with the construction of a lavish palace just for him. A Mannerist villa in style, part of it makes up the elegant, windowed green protuberance on the north side of Bolsena's old town. (Called the Palazzo del Drago, it's visitable by arrangement with the owner – 0761-799393.) Crispo was much enamoured of romantic details like chapels and passageways, and a legacy of this interest is apparent along the fascinating Via delle Piaggie which runs up behind his palace to the castle.

Bisentina Island

Although Bisentina Island certainly had a history before the Renaissance, it took on a particular importance in that period by virtue of the bigwigs who frequented the place and put up a few architectural gems. Every summer for a century or more, generations of Renaissance popes sighed and called this lovely island home.

And it *is* a lovely island. Some have described it as the most beautiful island on any lake in the world. Utterly quiet save for the breeze stirring the leaves of the oaks, willows, olive and bay trees, it offers a safe harbour to interesting wildlife uncommon elsewhere in the region (royal seagulls, herons, big black cormorants, beaver-like coypu, and so on). Girded with pale gold cliffs and carpeted with fragrant herbs, it is a little Garden of Eden – but better, because no snake can make it across the water to set up home here.

Bisentina isn't the lake's only island, of course. There's also nearby Martana Island, just over half as big at 10 hectares. Both are the heads of prehistoric volcanoes, made up of igneous rock and ejected cinders. They rise to a great height above the water surface, and share the distinction of having the lake's deepest part sited between them.

The name Bisentina has nothing to do with Byzantium or the Eastern Roman Empire, as many people assume. It comes from the Etruscan settlement of Vesentum or Bisentium which was once sited on the lakeshore nearby (see <u>Changing Places, Changing Names</u> section above). Etruscans were certainly burying their dead on the island as early as the 6th Century B.C., and it's thought that before they melded into the invading Roman population they used to flee here to escape Latin menace. They didn't know it, but they were the first in a long line of people who would use Bisentina Island as a place of retreat – of one kind or another. In the Dark Ages, people from various lakeside settlements would seek refuge on the island during Saracen invasions, while several centuries later men would seek long-term refuge there from the distractions of the material world. Men of pomp and power subsequently sought summer refuge there from the heat and political hassle of Rome.

The island's monastery went up in 1431, and for more than two centuries it witnessed the pieties and privations of Franciscan friars, Capuchin monks, and Camaldian hermits. Meanwhile, the immensely powerful Farnese family had arrived on the shores of Lake Bolsena, bringing with them peace and a new level of refinement – bringing the Renaissance, in fact, to lakeside towns still languishing in the Middle Ages. Jewel-like Bisentina Island certainly did not escape the Farneses' sophisticated notice, and it wasn't long before they were erecting an elegant church and several chapels there (the family was full of popes and cardinals, after all). Their church, built next to the monastery and dedicated to saints James and Christopher, has a wonderful domed octagonal tower which rises romantically out of surrounding foliage as you approach the island by boat. The chapels, charmingly tiny and set on high places, originally enabled summering clergy to recreate in miniature a sin-cleansing pilgrimage. At that time, one could obtain 'plenary indulgence' by travelling to seven different churches and then to St. Peter's in Rome. Churchmen at rest on Bisentina wanted this option of total absolution without the tedious business of leaving the island and interrupting their summer holiday. So they'd stroll round to Bisentina's seven chapels and end up in its one large church instead. Surely that was good enough? (It was if you were the pope, or the pope's pal.)

By the late 1600s, everyone had grown tired of Bisentina and the island was slowly abandoned. Buildings once shiny-new and humming with religious life crumbled quietly beneath the weight of passing centuries. Until 1912, when a princess bought up the whole place. She and her relatives would look after the island well, instigate building restoration, and allow the public limited access.

If you take advantage of this access and visit the island, it's likely to be on a boat trip run by Navigazione Alto Lazio (0761-798033 / 333-3819956). A schedule of trip departures is posted down at Bolsena's little port (by Piazzale Dante Alighieri). You can also pick up a leaflet at the Tourist Information Office or look at www.navigazionealtolazio.it. The final approach to the island by boat is enchanting, careering round a tall cliff topped with a little chapel before docking beside the island's main church – its walls a weathered patina of oranges, its ageing dome a patchwork of rusty greys. When you disembark, take a look at the old iron canopy built over the island's tiny port. It might be an eyesore, but it is also one of the world's first prefabricated structures, displayed at the 1911

International Exhibition in Turin before being dismantled and reassembled on the island. The stone sphinxes flanking it were added for gravitas by the purchasing princess. Your rightful instinct will be to roam freely round this beautiful island in a state of excitement, but you'll have to patiently follow the tour guide, I'm afraid.

Up to the Present

The 17th Century decline in interest in Bisentina Island coincided with a general abandonment of the much wider geographical area. Put plainly, northern Lazio and southern Tuscany slipped into depopulated obscurity for about three hundred years. This long-term lack of activity or investment is still reflected today in the area's number of cities, its general fame and level of tourist activity compared to other parts of Italy. But why the historical lapse in enthusiasm? The emergence of malarial swamps along the coast certainly didn't help, keeping the population low and repelling visitors (the swamps weren't fully eradicated until the 20th Century). Rome's fortunes had plummeted, which dried up much of the business traffic to and from the north. Meanwhile, ubiquitous thieves and highwaymen did their bit to deter casual passers-through. (A series of local routes, one of which skirts Lake Bolsena's western shore, are still called the *Sentieri dei Briganti* or 'Brigands' Paths'.) What few honest locals there were seemed content with subsistence farming and even with living in grass huts. Essayist Montaigne passing through in the 1580s and D.H. Lawrence visiting in the 1920s were both able to summarize the whole area as little more than a primitive wasteland.

In Bolsena itself, things never became too ugly or threadbare, just very, very quiet. Nothing remarkable seems to have gone on for a couple of centuries. Some excitement did come in 1815 when local people destroyed much of the town's castle to prevent Napoleon's brother Lucien seizing it. But once the damage had been done, no effort was made to undo any of it until the 20th Century.

The town started inching out of its torpor only in the late 1800s, around the same time that the myriad states and territories of Europe's boot-shaped peninsula were finally unified into a single nation. No doubt the sense of direction and identity instilled in newly-united Italians prompted town planners everywhere to think on a grander scale and build towards the future. One such was Bolsena magistrate Nicola Colesanti. Convinced that lake-bathing was good for health (an eccentric idea in those times), he proposed that a long, attractive avenue be built connecting central Piazza Matteotti to the lakeshore, enticing the Bolsenese to the beaches. Two hundred trees (mostly planes) were planted along the avenue and the shoreline so that bathers might stroll there and back in pleasant shade. Meanwhile, down on the water, the port was restored and the first passenger steamboat service began regularly crossing the lake. Grand villas and more modest homes would start going up – and all doing so much nearer the water than at any other time in the building of Bolsena. Modern notions of recreation and tourism had arrived, and a beautiful body of water was a valuable commodity, something to be as close to as possible.

Thus the three most active periods in Bolsena's history are distinctly associated with three separate areas of the town. What remains of the Etrusco-Roman settlement lies scattered across the upper hillside. The medieval network of narrow lanes sprawls across the lower hillside from the castle to Santa Cristina's Church. And the modern town thriving on tourism in particular laps along the very edges of the lake.

Colesanti would have been pleased to see how efforts continue towards making the lakeside more enticing for townsfolk and visitors. 21st Century gentrification projects include a miniature formal garden set up in Piazzale Dante Alighieri (I call the result 'God's Own Roundabout'). Elegant white balustrades topped with Classical urns have been erected along stretches of shoreline. And to further facilitate evening strolling, the port has been given a facelift and the area behind it paved and flanked with grass. There's a distinctly genteel flavour to these developments, underlining how the town wishes to be perceived and the kind of visitors it hopes to attract (the kind of visitors who will similarly appreciate the tasteful, low-rise hotels recently dotted along the shore). There are, for now, ample space and facilities in Bolsena for all those who visit. Visitor numbers can even expand without jeopardizing the calm and the natural beauty that draws people here in the first place. But the next few decades will prove critical, revealing whether or not the town's growing international popularity will continue to be successfully managed, as it is now, by careful planning and sensitive development.

PRACTICALITY

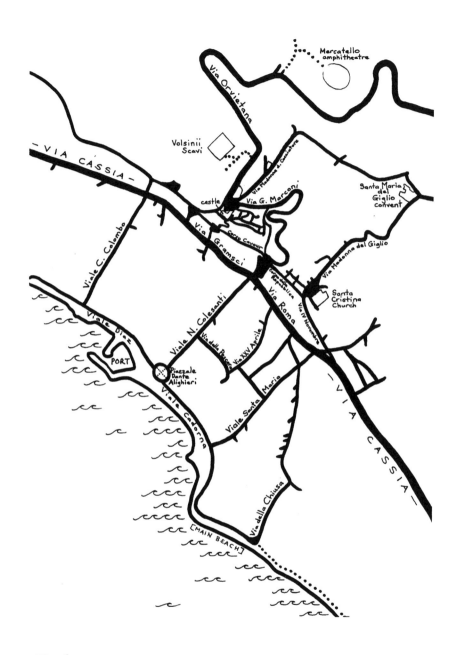

Bolsena

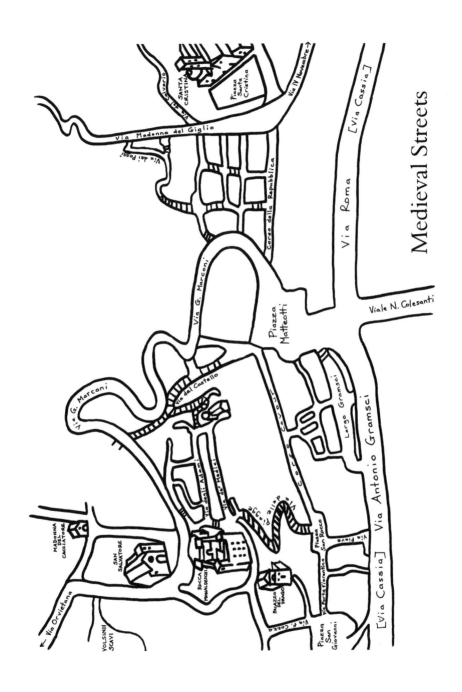

Medieval Streets

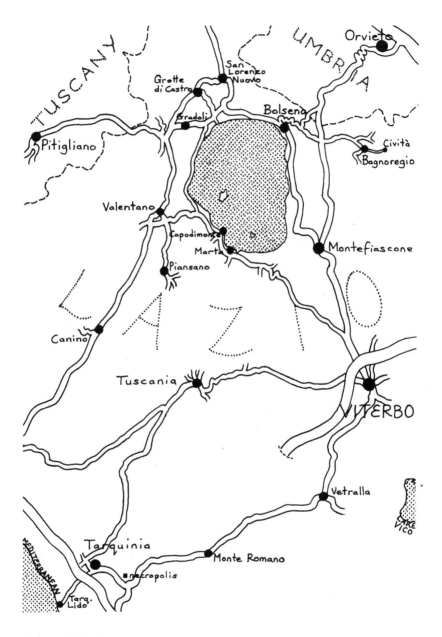

The Wider Area

FOOD AND DRINK

Eating in Italian Restaurants – some general notes

The Italian manner of eating can sometimes be vaguely reminiscent of the Cypriot *meze* system, where individual food items arrive separately on separate plates. Such gastronomic fragmentation can seem odd to diners from northern Europe, North America and the Antipodes accustomed to a single plate heaped high with meat and vegetables. Don't assume the service is bad in the restaurant you're in if, for example, you order fish, salad and chips and the three things arrive at different times. If you want to make certain everything comes at once, you might ask for this when you order, making use of *insieme* ('together') or phrases like *posso avere tutto alla stessa volta?* ('can I have everything at the same time?'). Bear in mind that things are deliberately served separately to allow you fully to savour each one of them and to prolong the meal, allowing it to become the main leisure activity of the evening. You are unlikely ever to feel rushed in an Italian restaurant, and you are usually very welcome to linger for as long as you like after you finish eating. (Indeed, it can sometimes be a struggle to get the bill.)

You'll notice that menus are generally divided into *antipasti* (starters), *primi piatti* (first courses – usually pasta or risotto), *secondi piatti* (second courses – usually meat or fish), *contorni* (side dishes, often served after the other courses), and so on. You are *not* obliged to have every course (!), and can freely pick and choose from all parts of the menu. In Italy, the distinctions between bar, café, and restaurant are often blurred, so you can usually arrive somewhere which serves food and just have drinks, or just have dessert, or just have chips if it takes your fancy to do so.

The Italians do not have an obsessive tipping culture, and when your bill includes *coperta* (cover charge) or *servizio* (service charge), you'll notice it's often not even quite 10% of the grand total. If your bill doesn't include such, tip at your own discretion of course.

All the aspects of restaurant dining outlined above should point to a single basic fact: in Italy, eating is seen as a fundamental pleasure, to be always as enjoyable and relaxed as possible. Restaurants have an *inclusive* atmosphere. Those who serve food are not demeaned by doing so, and those who eat in restaurants are not superior because they do so. Snobbery of any kind brings an unwelcome tension into the eating arena. And food snobbery, by the way, is unable to get much of a foothold in Italy because the food is so good everywhere – from the cheapest takeaway pizzeria to the most elegant city-centre restaurant. Why? Because of the optimum quality of basic ingredients. Whereas in France the food might be excellent thanks to the genius of the chef, in Italy it's excellent by virtue of the land, the climate, and the work of the farmer. It's a more elemental approach, one which can be said to glorify not so much the skill of man but the bounty of nature – a bounty which is obvious everywhere in this geographically blessed country.

One place where Italians fail to celebrate nature in their eating and drinking, however, is in their attitude to smoking. Non-smoking areas are rare in restaurants and non-existent in cafés and bars (despite utter fantasy talk of smoking being banned in public places). Thankfully, the majority of establishments have outdoor seating somewhere, and Italy's supremely hospitable climate makes it a pleasure to sit there for most of the year.

Restaurants – some recommendations

La Sirenetta ['the Little Mermaid'] 10 Viale Cadorna (lakeside)
0761-799096 (closed Mondays) €€
With a terrace overlooking the lake, La Sirenetta commands the best spot in Bolsena for watching the sunset. In summer the golden disc slots itself like a giant coin between mountains to the west. (Once it starts setting south of these, you know the season is moving on.) The food is simple but very good. I recommend the *Risotto alla Pescatora* (seafood rice) and the *Cipolline Balsamiche* (sweet onions pickled in balsamic vinegar).

Il Gabbiano ['the Seagull'] 2 Viale Cadorna (lakeside)
0761-799142 (closed Wednesdays) €€
Excellent simple food, and perhaps the best *coregone* in town (see Coregone section below). Outdoor dining is on a covered patio ringed with potted plants overlooking a private beach. If you're very lucky, some of the lake's more bolshy ducks might make hopeful sorties onto the premises. They prefer chips to bread, by the way.

La Pineta ['the Pinewood'] 48 Viale A. Diaz (lakeside)
0761-799801 (closed Mondays) €€€€ *non-smoking throughout*
Bolsena's swankiest restaurant, offering à la carte dining plus set lunchtime menus of creative things done with fish and seafood. I cannot recommend highly enough the show-stopping linguine with lobster and cherry tomatoes. The setting is quietly elegant and the atmosphere friendly and relaxed. Look out for the owners' gigantic black monolith of a dog, a Newfoundland named Arturo – comically attended by tiny Yorkshire Terriers.

La Tavernetta ['the Little Tavern'] 56 Corso Cavour (old town) 0761-798979 (closed Tuesdays) €
A snug little den in the heart of Bolsena's medieval lanes, with good food at rock-bottom prices. The pizzas are a marvel - delicious, crisp, and painfully filling. Far bigger than the giant plates, they lollop comically over the edges and drape across the tablecloths. The place is always well-attended, so they're obviously getting something right!

Trattoria del Moro ['the Moor's Restaurant'] Piazzale Dante Alighieri (lakeside) 0761-798810 (closed Thursdays) €€
Perched on wooden stilts in the water beneath a reed-thatched roof, this is a charming setting to enjoy simple, good-quality food and, if you're eating on the balcony, to toss the occasional piece of bread overboard and chuckle at the resulting pandemonium amongst the ducks. Eel (*anguilla*) is a speciality. Lake Bolsena's eels have long had wide repute; Dante mentions them in his *Divine Comedy* in a rant against gluttony (Purgatorio, XXIV). The Trattoria del Moro prepares them in a manner familiar to the poet: drowned in sweet vernaccia wine.

Bar Centrale Piazza Matteotti (old town) €€
Good pizzas and other dishes are served summer-only at outside tables perfect for people-watching and for a sense of being in the absolute heart of things.

Da Picchietto 15 Via Porta Fiorentina (old town) 0761-799158 (closed Mondays) €€
Good food has been served here for centuries – possibly for as many as seven of them.

Il Toscano ['the Tuscan'] 19 Via Gramsci (old town / main road) 0761-799054 (closed Tuesdays) €€
Good trattoria with the option of eating outside amidst tumbling wisteria at the right time of year.

Coregone

As you'd expect of a town with its toes in the water, there's always plenty of fish and seafood on restaurant menus in Bolsena. One word you'll find on almost every menu – but probably not in your Italian phrasebook or dictionary – is 'coregone'. Pronounced 'corray-GOAN-ay', this is the local word for the 'coregono' fish – which of course you haven't heard of either. A delicate, sensitive creature, it can only survive in very pure water. Naturally it thrives in Lake Bolsena. Delicious, plentiful, and emblematic of the lake's purity, the fish enjoys a great deal of local celebrity.

But it hasn't always been here. The species was introduced about 100 years ago from Lake Orta up in Lombardy. Introducing fish can be a risky business. The later introduction of trout into Lake Bolsena nearly spelt the end for the coregone, whose eggs and fry turned out to be delicious to trout. Coregone spawn is now collected and hatched in protected areas.

Mild and white-fleshed, coregone is similar to perch – but sweeter in taste and denser in texture. Unless you really detest fish, you can't visit Bolsena without trying this lovely foodstuff at least once. Being a revered local speciality, it's done extremely well everywhere – usually served roasted with a sprinkle of rosemary. I have to say I've consistently found it most mouthwatering at Il Gabbiano (see Restaurants above), where it comes with delectable singed bay leaves.

Snacks

Most café-bars in Bolsena serve bread-based snacks like hot and cold sandwiches, but there are also dedicated snackeries that serve hot food and dirt-cheap slices of good-quality pizza to eat in or take away. Look for *tavola calda* (hot table), *rosticceria* (roastery or roast meat shop) and *pizza a taglio* (pizza by the slice). There are places like this at 57 Corso della Repubblica, 10 Viale Colesanti, 10 Via Marconi, and 2-4 Via Piave. The café-bar Centrale in Piazza Matteotti also usually has a *tavola calda*.

Note that while vegetarians will have little problem, the growing number of people who choose to avoid wheat can have a tough time snacking in Bolsena. For example, most snack places that advertise chips rarely have any in practice. Your best bet is probably meat and vegetables at a *tavola calda* or *rosticceria*.

Ice cream

Ice cream was invented in Italy (the Romans were showing off bringing ice down from the Alps just to make a dessert), and Italian ice cream is still the best in the world. Now, far from being a luxury or indulgence, its status is something akin to a food staple, especially in the summer when it can seem almost an aid to survival in the heat. It's certainly not just for children or people in holiday mood. Stern-faced businessmen in sharp suits think nothing of crossing cities lapping at monstrous cones stuffed with multi-coloured dollops frilled with squirty cream.

In general, you should look out for phrases like "*gelato artigianale*" or "*produzione propria*" on the gelaterie you visit. These tell you that the ice cream is made on site, which usually gives a better product than the stuff that's mass-produced elsewhere and shipped in.

Bolsena is richly furnished with ice cream purveyors. All are up to the usual Italian standard, but one in particular deserves special mention. The enoteca-gelateria 'Santa Cristina' at 8 Corso della Repubblica has received accolades from the famous Slow Food Society for the quality and inventiveness of its produce.

Those seeking to avoid milk (or its calories) might like to know that there's a wide selection of gorgeous, milk-free sorbets at both the Blu Bar Gelateria (Viale N. Colesanti) and the Santa Cristina gelateria already mentioned. Santa Cristina also does soya milk, cholesterol-free and sugar-free ice creams.

Café-bars

There is rarely any discernible distinction between cafés and bars in Italy – both sell similar selections of drinks and do so at all times of the day and night. As the Italians rarely exhibit the over-enthusiasm for alcohol which sometimes bedevils northern Europeans, there are no restrictions on drinking such as licensing hours and the like. If you want to drink grappa at a café at 8 in the morning, it's your right to do so. (A well-dressed Italian would stop at *one* grappa, you see, not wishing to spoil his elegant clothes by falling down later.)

There is no culture of dedicated all-night alcohol consumption here. Thus at midnight on a Friday or Saturday, the atmosphere in Bolsena can seem that of a lively Sunday afternoon. People are as likely to be drinking coffee as spirits. Children run around playing, while teenagers, instead of withdrawing moodily among their own kind, sit happily outside at the same bars as the middle-aged. There is no War of the Generations in Italy, or at least not in Bolsena. All age groups do the same things – they go to restaurants, to café-bars, they go out for *passegiate*, they stay up late – and no one is 'uncool' for doing any of these things. They are universal pleasures.

As in the rest of Italy, you can't go more than a few paces in Bolsena without encountering a café-bar. They are the heart of social life, recreation, and private meditation. All Bolsena's café-bars are enjoyable places, and only a few deserve special mention by virtue of some unique characteristic they possess.

Bar del Moro Piazzale Dante Alighieri (lakeside – outdoor only)
Cheerful young women serve drinks here in leaf-dappled light next to a small, central beach. In the daytime, it's just about the most relaxing and convivial setting imaginable, and you can spend many hours here with absolutely no desire to be anywhere else.

Bar del Porto Piazzale Dante Alighieri (lakeside – outdoor only)
This café-bar shares the same beach as the Bar del Moro but offers several tables actually on the sand. The atmosphere is rather more youthful, with a jukebox and several table-football decks. (It's frequented by every age group, of course.) In the height of the summer, things really get jumping here at night: this is *the* place to be, and the buzzing fun goes on into the early hours.

Bar Centrale Piazza Matteotti (old town – indoor and outdoor)
As the name suggests, this place lies at the very heart of Bolsena and has something of the feel of a vital organ. In the summertime, its opening hours are nothing short of heroic, being something like 4am to 1:30am.

Tempio di Norzia 4 Largo Mazziotti (just north of old town's Piazza S. Giovanni – indoor and outdoor in summer)
Tucked away on an unassuming street just beyond the parts of town you're likely to explore is this extraordinarily stylish place

which looks and feels for all the world like a sleek Islington wine bar uprooted wholesale from London and dropped in Bolsena. You'll find pine tables, bold modern decor, a garrulous clientele, and a full and delicious menu served right up to the small hours. The name, incidentally, means 'Temple of Norzia' – Norzia being the Etruscan goddess of destiny, and a figure with a cult following in ancient Bolsena.

La Tanaquilla 100 Via G. Marconi (old town – indoor and outdoor)
Nestling behind buildings at the top of a flight of steps, the outdoor part of this pizzeria-pub has the feel of a Bavarian beer garden. It's open admirably late, and the high-backed wooden benches are flanked by overhead braziers to chase off any chill.

Coffee

In the Italian version of the reality television show *Survivor*, where starving contestants try to live on a deserted island with only the most basic and necessary tools for survival, the programme-makers didn't think it odd to provide the modern-day Robinson Crusoes with the means to make themselves perfect espresso every morning, served in a tiny china cup. Coffee, it seems, is an absolute necessity to an Italian – a fundamental without which all semblance of civilization breaks down, even in the middle of a jungle. You might take away proper beds and toilets and decent food and personal privacy, *but you can't take away coffee*. That would be barbaric. "Coffee is a *religion* here," an Italian once explained to me.

The number of café-bars in any Italian town should tell you that coffee is seen as a vital fixture in the business of living. And the fact that the Italians have coined so many terms for different ways of serving coffee – and spread those terms to the rest of the world – should tell you to what a high art they've perfected the stuff. Expect to be served a top quality drink in even the humblest-looking establishment. Here's a guide to the major types:

espresso (or simply **caffè**) – Tiny, black, and strong. Often knocked back like medicine.

caffè lungo – Espresso made slightly weaker and longer-lasting with a dash of hot water.

caffè americano – Espresso much weakened and enlarged with hot water.

caffè macchiato – Full-strength espresso with a dash of milk (hot, frothed, or cold).

cappuccino – Espresso topped with a thick head of steamed milk foam. The international darling of the Italian coffee scene.

caffè latte - Espresso weakened to americano proportions by hot liquid milk.

caffè corretto – Espresso enlivened by a dash of any spirit you fancy.

caffè freddo – Refreshing cold coffee.

caffè granita – Coffee with crushed ice, often topped with whipped cream.

And finally…

tè – Tea! Coffee has something of a monopoly in Italy and tea-as-the-English-know-it is rarely drunk here. You can get hot tea, of course, but it's usually served with lemon unless you specify you want milk (ask for a **tè con latte,** and expect a slightly raised eyebrow). Iced tea, especially with lemon or peach flavours, is immensely popular (ask for a **tè freddo**, and expect no eyebrow movement whatsoever).

Novel drinks

While you'll find lager and all the usual spirits available at Bolsena's café-bars, look out for Italian specialities like *grappa*, *limoncello*, *amaro*, *sambuca*, *Mirto di Sardegna*, *spumante dolce* and *prosecco*. *Grappa* is distilled vineyard leftovers (wine, leaves, grape skins, and so on). It's very strong and tastes of not much besides alcohol. Nice, though. *Limoncello* is a candy-coloured confection of lemons – sweet, strong, and skilfully just short of sickly. *Amaro* has a fascinating, multi-layered flavour that continues to develop after you've swallowed it. The name literally means 'bitter', but that's just one part of the taste's story. Italy's answer to Pernod and Ricard, *sambuca* is a sweet, aniseed-flavoured liqueur traditionally served set alight and with a floating coffee bean (but don't expect such tourist-indulging shenanigans in Bolsena). *Mirto di Sardegna* is a rather elegant Sardinian spirit made from myrtle berries. It's delicious, smelling and tasting something like a men's cologne. *Spumante dolce* is a sweet fizzing perfumed joy of a drink, whether you have it red (*rosso*) or white (*bianco*). If you'd prefer a dry, white version of this sparkling wine, ask for a *prosecco*.

On the subject of drinks, the most local white wine varieties to look out for in Bolsena include *Volsinio*, *Est Est Est* (properly written '*Est! Est!! Est!!!*', but I find that unjustifiably excited), and *Orvieto Classico* – all three decent but unexceptional. *Aleatico* from nearby Gradoli is a port-like dessert wine with lots of fruit and hints of spice. *Sangiovese* grapes are grown across a huge area of central Italy including northern Lazio and produce consistently pleasing, cherry-like stuff. Blended with *Ciliegiolo* (another cherry-like grape of the area) and *Aleatico*, *Sangiovese* can be exquisite. (They make this blend at the wonderful snack-cavern to the side of the main church in Bagnoregio's Civitá.) As Tuscany is so near to Bolsena, you should find no shortage of well-known reds like

Brunello and *Chianti*, as well as reds from other adjacent regions such as *Montepulciano d'Abruzzo* and so on.

ACCOMMODATION

(Please note: these are descriptions rather than reviews.)

Hotels
(all 3- and 4-star hotels listed here provide air conditioning and satellite television)

ROYAL ★★★★ 8-10 Piazzale Dante Alighieri (lakeside) 0761-797048
www.bolsenahotel.it/Royal/royal.html   royal@bolsenahotel.it
A venerable building with smart modern decor, set on the lakeside's central garden-piazza. 37 en suite rooms – the quietest overlooking a statue-lined swimming pool. Bar, lounges, shaded terrace, private parking.

HOLIDAY ★★★★ 38 Viale A. Diaz (lakeside) 0761-796900
www.bolsena.com   holiday@bolsena.com
Brand new hotel enjoying a quiet, spacious position next to the water. En suite rooms, many with balconies overlooking a line of lakeside umbrella pine trees. Large pool, lawns, restaurant, private parking.

NAIADI ★★★ 95 Viale Cadorna (lakeside) 0761-799017
www.bolsenahotels.it   naiadi@bolsenahotels.it
The only building looking onto Bolsena's main public beach. A stylish modern hotel with pool, garden, bar, restaurant, private parking, and en suite rooms with balconies.

COLUMBUS ★★★ 27 Viale Colesanti (lakeside) 0761-799009
www.bolsenahotel.it/columbus/columbus.html   columbus@bolsenahotel.it

Pleasant modern hotel opposite the Royal on the lakeside's central garden-piazza. 40 en suite rooms, varying in size and style, some with balconies looking onto allotments and gardens. Bar, restaurant.

NAZIONALE ★★★ 50 Via Gramsci (town centre) 0761-799006
www.hotelnazionale.net   info@hotelnazionale.net
Standing next to Bolsena's main crossroads, a large central hotel run by members of the same family for more than a century. Bar, terrace, gelateria, rooms with views of the castle.

EDEN ★★★ 46 Loc. Tempietto, Via Cassia (lakeside, out of town) 0761-799015
www.hoteledenbolsena.it   info@hoteledenbolsena.it
Small modern hotel on a private beach just outside Bolsena. A dozen or so en suite rooms, restaurant offering indoor and outdoor dining. Gardens, parking, pets welcome.

ZODIACO ★★★ 8 Via IV Novembre (old town) 0761-798791
www.primitaly.it/zodiaco   hotelzodiaco@tin.it
Just outside the old town gates, near Santa Cristina's Church, a completely refurbished early 20th Century building offering 12 rooms – some with balconies.

LORIANA ★★★ 33 Viale Cadorna (lakeside) 0761-799273 / 0761-799104
www.bolsenahotels.it   loriana@bolsenahotels.it
Modern hotel on the plane-tree-lined lakeside road. En suite rooms, pool, sun garden, bar, restaurant, gelateria, private parking.

AI PLATANI ★★★ Via Roma (town centre) 0761-799079
www.bolsena.com   platani@bolsena.com
Modern complex next to town centre's main crossroads. En suite rooms, some with balconies. Garden, terrace-solarium, bar, restaurant, private parking.

LIDO ★★★ Via Cassia (lakeside, out of town) 0761-799026
www.bolsenahotel.it/hotel_lido/lido.html   lido@bolsenahotel.it
Small modern hotel set on its own beach outside town. 12 en suite rooms with private terraces. Garden, restaurant.

ITALIA ★ Corso Cavour (old town) 0761-799193
A handful of bargain rooms sited in the very heart of Bolsena's
medieval pedestrian lanes. Rooftop terrace with panoramic views.
Some rooms en suite.

B&Bs, self-catering apartments, and 'agriturismi' – farmhouses with rooms or apartments

MONTEBELLO Via Orvietana 0761-798965
www.lariservamontebello.com   marcozammarano@libero.it
agriturismo@lariservamontebello.com
Large stone farmhouse with pool and lake views set on wooded
hillside just outside Bolsena. En suite rooms with antique furniture.
Local produce; regional and international dishes.

L'ANTICA FATTORIA Via Cassia 0761-799166 / 347-360-6679
www.lanticafattoria.it   pagliacciamauro@tin.it   mauropagliaccio@libero.it
Refurbished 19th Century farmhouse in country park setting 300m
from the lakeshore, 3km south of Bolsena's centre. 7 holiday
apartments sharing pool and private beach. Local produce, especially
honey and beeswax.

TARA Via Cassia 0761-799278
selvale@libero.it
Family-run bed and breakfast with 4 double rooms on the southern
edge of the town centre, 5 minutes' walk from the lake. Traditional
home cooking.

IL MURACCIO Loc. Muraccio, Via Cassia 0761-799005 /
0761-780854 / 338-483-7774 / 368-340-1655
www.muraccio.it   info@muraccio.it   agriturismo.muraccio@virgilio.it

3km from Bolsena and 100m from a private beach, an old stone farmhouse offering apartments with private entrances – one fully equipped to accommodate disabled visitors. Pets welcome.

BELVEDERE Via Orvietana 0761-798290

www.paginegialle.it/agriturismopuri   agriturismopuri@inwind.it
info@agritouristbelvedere.it

12 en suite rooms in a hillside setting with views of the lake. Restaurant serving local food and produce.

LA PIANTATA Via Cassia 0761-799794

www.turismoverde.it/guida2003/lazio/lapiantata.htm

Bungalow set in 10 hectares of land near lake offers 1 single and 2 double rooms, all en suite. Home cooking and local produce.

AL CASTELLO 11 Via del Castello 0761-799534 / 328-666-2263
Small bed and breakfast situated on the pedestrian climb up to Bolsena's most atmospheric medieval alleyways.

PODERACCIO Via Cassia 0761-798443 / 0761-799594 /
338-610-9431

www.primitaly.it/agriturismo/poderaccio   poderaccio@primitaly.it

Grand refurbished villa with four apartments on a spacious farm estate overlooking lake, 2km west of Bolsena's centre.

VILLA STELLA / PONY CLUB / COLLINA BLU
Loc. Biagio, Via Orvietana 0763-28485 / 333-293-0818
www.worlditalia.com/umbria/terni/collinablu
www.primitaly.it/villeecasali/villastella/uk.htm (e-mail via both websites)
Right on the Lazio-Umbria border, 5km from Bolsena in rolling hills overlooking the lake, an 18th Century stone farmhouse offering B&B rooms. Pool, horse riding, English-style gardens, and dining room with impressive vaulted ceiling.

LE VIGNE Loc. Vigne 0761-799875 / 333-996-5878
www.levigne.it   info@levigne.it
En suite rooms with private entrances in rural setting just outside town centre on hillside overlooking lake. Local food.

LA FRASCHETTA Via Cassia 0761-799678 / 0761-798059
www.lagodibolsena.it/agriturismi/lafraschetta.html
Self-contained apartments in 12 hectares of fruit groves, 100m from the lakeshore.

PODERE ARLENA Via Cassia 0761-799538 / 333-937-8769
www.arlena.it   info@arlena.it   agriturismo@arlena.it
8 apartments 4km south of Bolsena. 150m path through fruit groves to a private beach. Local fruit, oil and wine sold.

DOLCE VITA Loc. Piantata, Via Cassia 0761-797074 / 0761-798519
www.agriturismodolcevita.it   info@agroturismodolcevita.it
Bungalow apartments 400m from the lake, amidst orchards west of Bolsena. Pool, garden.

PODERNOVO Loc. Podernovo, Via Cassia 0761-798514
www.holidaysinumbria.com/podernovo   podernovo@libero.it
Grand 19th Century stone farmhouse, fully refurbished, on large estate with wide views over the lake. 3 apartments, 1km from the water.

LORY 2 Via della Pescara 0761-799104
Small bed and breakfast on a quiet street running alongside allotments halfway between the lakeside and Bolsena's medieval centre.

IL CASALE DEL CONTADINO Loc. Melone, Via Cassia
0761-799816 / 349-475-1427 / 338-837-2555
www.bolsena.info/html/it/objekte/contadino2   massimobruti@inwind.it
Two lakeside apartments 2.5 km from Bolsena. Terraces, small garden, pool.

VILLA PIOPPETA Via Cassia 0761-824751 / 329-421-7768
www.primitaly.it/villeecasali/pioppeta/uk.htm   angeloferlicca@libero.it
Large restored stone and stucco farmhouse near the lakeshore, 1km outside Bolsena. 3 apartments with private entrances. Large garden, private beach.

LE PALME Via Cassia 0761-799671 / 335-619-9908
www.agriturismolepalme.it   info@agriturismolepalme.it

Apartments in farmhouse villa set on hillside with lake views. Pool, garden, large restaurant with fireplace. Local produce, especially home-grown fruit and vegetables.

Also see LIDO, MASSIMO, and VAL DI SOLE in Campsites, below.

Convent rooms

CONVENTO SANTA MARIA DEL GIGLIO 49 Via Madonna del Giglio 0761-799066 *www.conventobolsena.org*   *puntivista@pelagus.it*
By renting out very simple single and double rooms at rock-bottom prices, this 17th Century convent can afford to restore and maintain its cloistered, frescoed premises. Set amidst vineyards and olive groves on a hillside with lake views, the town and the water are a pleasant walk away. Guests can pay a small supplement to use the kitchen and dining room.

Campsites

LIDO ★★★★ Via Cassia 0761-799258 / 0761-797048
www.bolsenacamping.it/camping-lido/camping.html
lidocamping@bolsenahotel.it
Large, orderly campsite offering every facility on a private stretch of beach 1km south of Bolsena. Town reachable by road or lakeside footpath. Pool, bar, restaurant, supermarket, disco, cinema, games room, tennis courts. Apartments, bungalow and mobile homes also available on site.

MASSIMO ★★★ Via Cassia 0761-798738
www.massimo.info   *heinz.reul@t-online.de*   *massimo.bolsena@libero.it*

A bit of everything 3.5km from Bolsena. Small campsite, 4 apartments, 2 studios, 2 chalets, 2 bungalows. Sandy beach, shady grounds, bar-trattoria with local dishes.

BLU INTERNATIONAL ★★★ Via Cassia 0761-799197 / 0761-798855
www.blucamping.it   info@blucamping.it
Medium-sized campsite facing a fine black beach in the midst of fruit groves and rustic fishermen's huts. Bolsena 1km away by road or lakeside footpath. Supermarket, bar, pizzeria with regional dishes.

IL LAGO ★★★ 6 Viale Cadorna 0761-799191 / 0761-798498
www.campingillago.it   info@campingillago.it
Very small site on the main lakeside boulevard, 400m from town centre. Private beach, pizzeria. All Bolsena's restaurants on your doorstep.

CAPPELLETTA ★★ Via Cassia 0761-799543 / 0761-799158
Space for about 100 tents 3.5 km from Bolsena. Beach, supermarket, bar, hot table.

VAL DE SOLE (star rating unknown) Via Cassia 0761-799012 / 0761-797064
www.primitaly.it/camping/valdisole/index.html   valdisole@virgilio.it
Large campsite and 11 bungalows next to a beach backed by woods 5km northwest of Bolsena. Bar, supermarket, restaurant with garden serving local dishes and home-grown produce.

PINETA ★★ Viale A. Diaz 0761-799801 / 0761-798447
Small campsite nestling in a quiet corner next to Bolsena's smartest restaurant. On the lakeside about 500m from the town centre.

ROMANTIC CHEZ VOUS (star rating unknown) Via Cassia 0761-798738 / 0761-799557
Beachside campsite outside Bolsena. Supermarket, hot table.

SHOPPING AND SERVICES

Opening hours

Central Italy takes siesta. Expect shops to be open from around 9am to 1pm then again from 4 or 5pm till 7 or 8pm. In Bolsena, many shops remain closed on Thursday afternoons.

Clothes

Incredible bargains can be had at *I Re Pazzi* ('The Mad Kings') at 37 Corso della Repubblica. Various boutiques are located in the same street, in Piazza Matteotti, on Corso Cavour and the streets running off it. For sports clothes, try *Bolsena Yachting* at 4a Via Gramsci. For haute couture, investigate *Sartoria Alessia* in Piazza San Rocco.

Shoes

Shops on Corso della Repubblica, on Corso Cavour, and in Piazza Matteotti.

Giftshops

Classy, interesting stuff can be acquired at no. 24 Corso della Repubblica, while gourmet items can be bought at Santa Cristina enoteca-gelateria (no. 8). Pretty ceramics are sold at 66 Corso della Repubblica, while rather more dramatic fired ware is available at *Terre di Rasenna*, tucked away at no. 12 Via Donzellini off the Corso Cavour. Bright – but not tacky – souvenir ceramics are sold at a kiosk next to the Bar del Porto on Piazzale Dante Alighieri. Wooden objects and collector toys come from 68 Corso della Repubblica; herbal things and original perfumes come from no. 4 on the same street.

Markets

Tuesdays till 1pm in Piazza Matteotti, and summer Sundays till 5-ish along Viale Cadorna on the lakeside.

Groceries

As a visitor in an unfamiliar town, you'd be forgiven for heading straight to a supermarket rather than traipsing round trying to find individual food shops. Bolsena's supermarkets are at 38 Via XXV Aprile, 14 Via Piave (corner of Via Gramsci), and on the Via Cassia at the top of Viale C. Colombo. However, shopping for foodstuffs in the happy hubbub of the main shopping thoroughfares is such a convivial pleasure, with all the shopkeepers standing outside chatting and calling hello to each other, that I recommend it if at all possible. Grocers (*alimentari*), butchers (*macelleria*), and bakers (*panetteria*) have numerous shops on Corso Cavour, Corso della Repubblica, and in Piazza Matteotti. Fishmongers (look for *pesce*) can be found in Piazza San Rocco and next to Il Toscano restaurant on Via Gramsci (no. 27). Fruit and vegetable shops (*frutta e verdura*) are everywhere, but I particularly recommend the little shop at the end of Corso della Repubblica (no. 74) near Santa Cristina's Church. The fruit and vegetables here, in my experience, are consistently the tastiest in Bolsena. The owner grows some of them himself.

Drink (and wine-tasting)

For beer, wine, and soft drinks, try the *Enoteca Mariottini* at 32 Viale Colesanti as well as local supermarkets. For fine wine, visit Santa Cristina enoteca-gelateria at 8 Corso della Repubblica, and for evening and late-night wine-tasting in a wonderfully atmospheric setting, do visit *Ænos* up on Piazza della Rocca next to the castle. The owner is admirably passionate about wine and can talk to you about it in very good French if you can't keep up the Italian, especially after a few glasses. His premises have historical interest and include two ancient, possibly Etruscan, cellars he personally had excavated. They are neat, temple-like places lit by honey-scented candles. One contains an original votive altar, focus for a congregation of wine bottles.

Photographic, Electrical, Opticians, Hairdressers, Haberdashery

There is at least one of each on the two main shopping streets, Corso della Repubblica and Corso Cavour. A men's barber operates on Via Piave.

Chemist's / Pharmacy

Next door to the Post Office on Via Gramsci. 0761-799031

Newspapers

Foreign-language newspapers, including British and American ones, can be bought in the large green metal kiosk at the corner of Via Gramsci and Viale Colesanti, and in the shop with *"Edicola"* written above it in Piazza Matteotti. Expect to pay about three times the price you're used to at home.

Internet access

Of public places to access the internet, one is the most reliable: the print and copy shop with "FAX" and "PHOTOCOPIE" written on it, halfway along Corso della Repubblica (no. 26). You can also try your luck at the Tourist Information Office, and at *La Libreria* at 1 Via Porta Fiorentina. If you're staying in a hotel, many have computers guests can pay to use.

Post Office

Next to the Hotel Nazionale/*Banco di Brescia*, just to the north of Via Gramsci's junction with Viale Colesanti. Open every weekday until 2pm and Saturdays until 1pm. 0761-799018

Tourist Information Office

9 Piazza Matteotti. 0761-799923. (Can be hit and miss in usefulness.)

Cashpoints

(1.) Outside the *Banco di Brescia* next to the traffic lights at the junction of Via Gramsci and Viale Colesanti; (2.) outside the *Cassa di Risparmio di Orvieto* in Piazza Matteotti; (3.) on the wall of the Post Office.

Public Phones

Bolsena is poorly stocked with the working variety of these. Pristine, tempting booths often turn out to have no phone inside. Perhaps you're meant to use your mobile in them. Actual phones can be found inside the booths on Largo (Via) Gramsci, opposite the Post Office. There's one on Piazza San Giovanni, and one next to the Bar del Moro down on the lakeside.

Public Toilets

No great bounty of these either. In the old town, there's a set on Via IV Novembre and another on Vicolo de Lavatoio not far from the castle. Both are very clean (but rarely have toilet paper). Down on the lakeside, a staffed public toilet operates in a yellow hut (not the one with the fence around it) on the corner of Viale Cadorna and Viale Santa Maria, near the Hotel Loriana.

EMERGENCIES

Emergency phone numbers

112 – police (*Carabinieri*)
113 – any emergency service, including ambulances
115 – fire brigade (*Vigili del Fuoco*)
116 – roadside assistance (*Soccorso Stradale*)
118 – medical emergencies (*Pronto Soccorso*)

Direct numbers in Bolsena

0761-8331 – medical emergencies (*Pronto Soccorso*)
339-291-7107 / 339-180-4594 – ambulance
0761-799002 – police (*Carabinieri*)
0761-798771 – police (*Polizia Municipale*)

"Parla inglese?"
[PAR-la een-GLAY-zay?]
'Do you speak English?'
"C'e qualcuno che parla inglese?"
[Chay kwall-KOO-no kay PAR-la een-GLAY-zay?]
'Is there anyone there who speaks English?'

Crime and the Police

There is virtually no crime in Bolsena and you should feel very, very safe here. Should you ever need them, the Carabinieri have a station on Via XXV Aprile. The fact that the building is painted pink and festooned with flowers should tell you something about the seriousness of offences expected in Bolsena. Both the Polizia Municipale and the Carabinieri make regular, reassuring patrols round the town on foot and by car.

Doctors and Hospitals

Bolsena's doctors' surgery is on Via IV Novembre and opens only on Mondays, Wednesdays and Fridays, from 3 to 5pm in summer and from 5 to 7pm in winter (0761-798178 or 330-310606). The nearest hospital (*ospedale*) is 20 minutes away in Montefiascone (well-signposted once you reach the town. 0761-798869). The nearest *big* hospital is 40 minutes away in Orvieto (again, well-signposted). The Italian equivalent of Casualty / A & E / Emergency Room is *Pronto Soccorso*. You will be treated more or less immediately (unlike, alas, in Britain), and EU citizens will not be charged a thing.

EXPLORATION

RECOMMENDED WALKS

Walk 1. Medieval Bolsena

Summary:

A half-hour wander through old Bolsena's narrow cobbled lanes and alleyways, with a couple of great views over the town. This walk is particularly atmospheric taken at night.

Detailed directions:

start: Piazza Matteotti

With the Tourist Information Office behind you, go to the piazza's top left corner and pass through a large brown stone arch where a small sign promises "*centro storico negozi*" ('old town shops'). This street is the Corso Cavour and you follow it for about 2 or 3 minutes until it opens out onto the little Piazza San Rocco with its Renaissance fountain and basins. With the fountain ahead of you, turn sharply right at the edge of the yellow building housing *Sartoria Alessia* and begin climbing steps leading through an archway. This is the Via delle Piaggie ('street of the staircase'). Note the thin Roman brickwork at the bottom of the wall straight ahead of you as you go under the archway. As the alley climbs up and up, you'll pass through a strange corridor with a high, vaulted ceiling which looks like the nave of an abandoned church (the work of Tiberio Crispo, as mentioned in <u>Medieval and Renaissance Bolsena</u>). Note the dome and interesting chimneypots a little further on.

After 4 or 5 minutes' climbing, you emerge into the joined Piazza dell'Orologia and Piazza della Rocca, with the castle on your left. Turn right into Via de' Medici. After a minute or so, you'll meet a tiny staggered crossroads. Turn right and walk to the little stone balcony at the alley's end to catch a great view of Bolsena. When you've seen enough, turn round and walk straight over the crossroads, down the short alley that *was* on your left when you were on the Via de' Medici. Turn left at the alley's end onto Via degli Adami. Seconds later, take the first right into the Via del Lavatoio ('street of the public washhouse'). Follow it for a minute or two, curving to the left, and passing en route the *lavatoio* in question on the right, some public toilets, and going through a long, low archway.

At the stone table and chairs, take the staircase ahead and slightly to the right. Emerge into the car park of the Piazza della Rocca and take the first left, putting the castle to your right. Turn left again where a vintage sign points to *"Alimentari Tabacchi"* ('foodshop, tobacconist'), putting you once more on the Via degli Adami. Go straight ahead for 2 minutes and descend through an archway. Where the steps make a hairpin bend to the left, go right to another stone balcony and admire a slightly different view of Bolsena. Turn back and carry on down the steps, which soon curve round to the right. You'll find yourself back in Piazza Matteotti in a couple of minutes, but just where the steps change into a cobbled slope, don't forget to look back at the view of the old town rising haughtily above you.

Walk 2. Reed Tunnels and Black Beaches

Summary:
A lovely hour-long stroll showcasing Bolsena's elemental beauty. After a tree-lined lakeside boulevard, you follow a path through towering bamboo-like reeds past tiny beaches of sparkling dark grey sand. Examine a handful of this sand (much finer than on Bolsena's main beaches) and you'll see it's made up of green, black,

76

and colourless filaments of volcanic glass. The walk leads past fruit trees and fishermen's huts, and includes a short diversion to the intriguing *Pietre Lanciate* ('thrown stones') – a wall of ancient lava which cooled into sprouting prisms of rock.

Detailed directions:
start: Piazzale Dante Alighieri
Facing the lake, take the road leading left along the lakeside, Viale Cadorna. For about 10 minutes you'll be strolling in leaf-dappled light thronging mottle-barked plane trees – the shade enabling your eyes to better appreciate the blue of the lake. Just follow the road as far as you can go, passing Il Gabbiano restaurant and an urn-topped white balustrade on the right, the Hotel Loriana and Viale Santa Maria on the left, then the Il Lago campsite and La Sirenetta restaurant on the right. The road will curve and cross a little bridge before revealing the town's main beach stretching away from the Hotel Naiadi.

Carry on beside the beach to a little roundabout, where a road coming from the left is labelled Via della Chiusa. Go straight ahead onto an unsurfaced track heading off into bamboo-like reeds along the water's edge, going round the white barrier if it's across your path. On the left you'll be passing the first of many olive groves; on the right, look out for tiny beaches of dark volcanic sand spaced at intervals between the reeds. These reeds arch overhead and form tunnels wherever the path narrows. After about 7 minutes, you have to cross a tiny stream unless exceptionally hot weather has dried it away. The little dirt trail to the right offers a slightly easier crossing. After another 5 minutes and a series of fishermen's huts (where lake fishermen take up full-time summer residence with their families), a small surfaced road joins your path from the left. This is where you'll make an interesting diversion on your return leg, but for now carry on straight ahead, passing the Blu International campsite on your left.

After a couple of minutes, you come to an open gateway in a mesh fence, overlooking a small drop onto a stream. This icy-cold little stream might not look anything special, but it acts like an international border – marking the end of things Italian and the start of things Teutonic. Across the stream is the extremely well-run Lido Camping Village, populated almost exclusively with German and Dutch holidaymakers. Suddenly everyone is taller and blonder than you've grown used to in Bolsena. Women sunbathe topless (culture shock no. 1), and *no one takes any notice of them* (culture shock no. 2). The children behave differently too. Whereas the *bambini* of Bolsena run guilelessly around enthralled by the elements, these kids busy themselves with toys, devices, with miniature machines, and in building lakeside dams – like so many engineers-in-waiting. Call me a shameful peddler of tired old stereotypes if you like, but the sudden transition can be startling.

Bearing in mind that you are entering the temporary home of paying guests and behaving therefore with all due consideration, cross the stream and trot inconspicuously along the water's edge for several seconds to where it curves out into a little projection of rocks. Look behind you for a magical view of Bolsena nestling amidst the hills, its tall medieval buildings sprouting like a tight cluster of mushrooms on the otherwise green landscape. Now go back exactly the way you came, along the beach and up over the boundary stream.

When you meet the small tarmacked road joining your path from the right on the corner of Blu International campsite, turn up it and progress for 5 minutes until you come to the main road (Via Cassia). On the other side of this road you should already be able to see a curious wall of rock where stone sprouts upwards in crystal-like polyhedrons. If you'd like to take a closer look and to read the interesting bumf posted on an information board, cross the road *with extreme care*, bearing in mind that traffic on this stretch is infrequent but fast. Afterwards, go back down the little road you came up on, turn right when you rejoin the lakeside path at the bottom, and retrace your steps through the reed tunnels, past the black beaches, and through the leaf-dappled light of the lakeside road.

Walk 3. Town and Country

Summary:
A 40-minute ramble taking in country lanes flanked with vines and olive trees, passing a hilltop convent, and descending through residential alleys offering wonderful views over Bolsena's sprawl of terracotta rooftops.

Detailed directions:
start: Piazza Matteotti
With the Tourist Information Office behind you, go to the piazza's top left corner and make your way up the cobbled slope (becoming shallow stone steps) situated between the brown stone archway and the deconsecrated church with the attractive doorway. This is the Via del Castello ('street of the castle'). After about 3 minutes' climbing (don't take the sharp left turn halfway up), you should emerge onto the main road, Via G. Marconi. Turn left and continue on to the car park of the Piazza della Rocca (next to the castle), 2 minutes away. Turn right to face the large church of San Salvatore (the one with the simple rose window and the half-figure of Christ over the doorway). Take the small road running immediately right of this church, the Via Madonna del Cacciatore, and continue for 2 minutes until you reach the tiny 15th Century church of Madonna del Cacciatore ('Madonna of the Hunter'). If the doors aren't locked, take a peek inside at the frescos depicting

San Rocco. Putting this little church on your left, carry on along a pale gravel track flanked by a vineyard and an olive grove. This type of rough country road is found all over rural Italy and is referred to as *strada bianca* ('white road').

After a couple of minutes, the track will curve sharply to the right, and after another 4 minutes or so its surface will change to asphalt. Enjoy the lovely glimpses of Bolsena and the lake through the silvery-green olive leaves. After about 4 minutes of tarmacked progress toward the convent of Santa Maria del Giglio ('Saint Mary of the Lily'), you meet a T-junction at which you should turn right and begin travelling downhill, putting the convent immediately on your right. The downhill road, which you should follow for 8 or 9 minutes, winds its way past rockfaces and the occasional house.

Look out for the first available right turn (a street, not a driveway), which has a sign declaring "*strada senza uscita*" ('street without exit'). This is the Via dei Poggi ('street of the hillocks'), and you should climb it for about 10 seconds before turning left onto a flat stretch which eventually curves to the right. All along this stretch are glorious views of Santa Cristina's Church and the undulating terracotta rooftops of Bolsena. Follow the path round for a couple of minutes, and you'll emerge onto a set of cobbled steps leading down to the left. Descend them for a minute between flower-decked homes until a little road meets you from the left and a sign reading "*Largo Parione*" can be seen on the building ahead of you. Turn right here, meeting some steps after a few seconds and going down them to come out onto the main road. Turn left and follow the road round to find yourself back in Piazza Matteotti. Have an ice cream or a coffee and reflect on what a sense of perspective you've gained on Bolsena!

RECOMMENDED BIKE RIDES

Ride 1. Halfway Round the Lake

Summary:

An easygoing roll along the lake's western edge, with constant beautiful views of the water, the opposite shores, and Bisentina Island. The tarmacked country road is flanked by small fields of crops, olive groves, and occasional picnic areas. Opportunities for swimming are boundless, and opportunities for snacking are provided by several tiny cafés. The route can take you as far as Capodimonte, an extremely pretty little town with fewer than 2,000 inhabitants set on a high wooded promontory overlooking the lake. (You'll see the octagonal Renaissance castle rising over the water long before you reach the town. And this Capodimonte is *not* the home of the porcelain trinkets, in case you're wondering. They come from an eponymous area of Naples.) Note that the first 4 miles (6km) of this route are, unavoidably, along the Via Cassia – the quite fast but not overcrowded main road leaving Bolsena. Those able to transport their bicycles in another vehicle along the Via Cassia before beginning their ride on the route's most pleasant central stretch might want to consider doing so.

Maximum distance:

15 miles there + 15 miles back = 30 miles (48 km). This distance can be reduced as much as desired, by not going all the way to Capodimonte, and/or by driving your bicycle/s out of Bolsena first.

Detailed directions:

Join the Via Cassia heading northwest out of Bolsena. After about 4 miles (6km), there's a turning to the left with a bank of yellow signposts. Ignore it, and hold on for the turning just beyond it, with a bank of *blue* signposts (pointing towards Gradoli, etc.). This is the SS489, and you should follow it for about 2 miles (3 km) before taking a turn to the left signposted 'Capodimonte'. If you're on a bike, the cycling will get lovelier from this point onwards. If you're in a vehicle, park somewhere soon and continue on two wheels (there's a suitable barren patch on the left a short distance after you make this turn toward Capodimonte).

After cycling for 5 beautiful miles (8 equally beautiful km), the road surfacing ends and it can be a bit bumpy for the next mile while you travel beside a long, straight beach. As soon as the tarmac returns, you're faced with climbing the route's only hill, Monte Bisenzio – once the site of an Etruscan town. You might wish to turn back at this point. If you want to carry on to Capodimonte, climb the hill and follow the little road until you reach a T-junction, where you should turn left. This is a fairly fast road, but extremely wide with lots of room for cyclists. Less than 2 miles later, take the signposted left turn into Capodimonte and continue for a mile or so to reach the heart of this pretty little town. Once there, I recommend getting off the bike and wandering round the tiny old streets spread across the high promontory.

To get back to Bolsena, simply go back the way you came. There's no easy way of carrying on for a full circuit of the lake, I'm afraid.

Ride 2. Bolsena to Cività di Bagnoregio

Summary:
This is an energetic cycle in its early stages because you have to climb out of Bolsena's volcanic crater. For 6½ km (4 miles), you'll wind steadily (but never steeply) uphill on a road with modest

traffic and glorious views across the lake. (Cyclists able to transport their bikes in a car or van might like to consider cheating and beginning their ride at the crossroads beyond the crater's rim – cutting out all the route's uphill slog as well as its final downhill whizz.) The crater conquered, there follows some wonderful cycling across lyrical countryside. The tarmacked country roads see very little traffic and the rolling farmland spools prettily past. You'll travel by silent cropfields and idyllic-looking farmhouses, admire the corduroy of vineyards arcing across the land, before the road winds through woods and carves between strange rockfaces. Riders familiar with Umbria will note that the landscape and rich brown soil on the post-crater section are distinctly reminiscent of a region which is, after all, no more than 3 km away at any point on this journey. The final stretch takes you through the handsome town of Bagnoregio to reach its main attraction, the spectacular Cività (see description in <u>Trip 3</u> of the RECOMMENDED EXCURSIONS BY CAR, below). Once at Cività, you'll probably want to lock up the bikes and wander open-mouthed across the bridge to explore it.

Maximum distance:
14.7 km there + 14.7 km back = 29.4 km (just over 18 miles). Drivers beginning their cycling at the hilltop crossroads can expect to ride 8.2 km there + 8.2 km back = 16.4 km (10 miles).

Detailed directions:
From Piazza Matteotti, follow the main Via Marconi winding up out of town, passing the castle and the *Volsinii Scavi* site on the left. Carry on for 6½ km (4 miles) along this twisting uphill road, the main route east out of Bolsena. Ignore protesting leg muscles and admire the fabulous views across the lake. Remind yourself that you're climbing out of a huge volcanic crater. After most of the climbing is over, go past a signposted turning for Orvieto on the

left and carry straight on towards Bagnoregio (also signposted). At the bottom of a short downhill stretch, you'll meet a crossroads with a major road, the SS71. Those driving their bicycles out of the crater should park somewhere hereabouts and start cycling.

Cross the main road *with extreme care* and carry on straight ahead. Bagnoregio is meticulously signposted from here and you cannot miss it (especially as there is only one fork in the road in the next 6 km / 4 miles of beautiful countryside). Once in Bagnoregio itself, you'll pass a large supermarket on the right and come to a T-junction. Go to the left and look out for a large, free-standing arch or city gate in the middle of a sort of traffic piazza on the right. This is the Porta Albana, and it looks slightly ridiculous denuded of city walls on either side. Go to the right of the arch and continue along the road through the town, following all signs to Città. There'll be a signposted 90° turn right just as the townhouses start to thin out and you'll curve round a downhill road with a spacious landscape appearing on your right before Città suddenly looms gobsmackingly ahead of you.

Exploring Città takes an hour or so. (To get the best of it, refer to the last four paragraphs of Trip 3 in the RECOMMENDED EXCURSIONS BY CAR.) Getting back to Bolsena is a simple matter of retracing your route out. At one point going back through Bagnoregio you'll be obliged to turn right in keeping with the town's modest one-way system. You'll eventually emerge at the Porta Albana once more. Bolsena is well signposted all the way home.

Note: *Really* keen cyclists for whom Bolsena is just one town on a large cycling itinerary might like to know that it's possible to carry on from Bagnoregio across similarly attractive terrain and quiet roads all the way to Orvieto. Simply follow signs to Orvieto rather than to Bolsena once you've come back through the main part of Bagnoregio to the Porta Albana. Orvieto is 15.6 km (9½ miles) from here.

Ride 3. Reed Tunnels and Black Beaches

My recommended walk no. 2 can easily be done by bicycle in a leisurely half-hour or so. With the added height of a bike and the increased speed of being on two wheels, it can be great fun ducking out the way of the overarching reeds. The off-road surface is a mixture of dirt and packed sand, so you shouldn't struggle too much. Just watch out for walkers and always give them right of way.

Hiring bikes in Bolsena

Try La Spiaggetta, on the lakeside at 2 Viale Cadorna. 0761-798536

RECOMMENDED EXCURSIONS BY CAR

Trip 1. Orvieto (15 miles / 24 km)

Spectacularly set on a table of rock rising into the sky from a lushly fertile valley-plain, Orvieto is a perfectly preserved medieval city full of elegant, gingerbread-coloured buildings. It's also home to what Italians judge to be the most beautiful cathedral in Italy – a black-and-white-striped megalith with a show-stopping multi-coloured facade. The approach by road from Bolsena allows you *the* most stunning views of Orvieto as you wind down a series of hairpin bends scored into an adjacent hillside. Just try not to crash the car while you're gasping at the magnificence beyond the window.

With its stunningly strategic position atop what was once the molten core of an erupting volcano, it's easy to understand why Orvieto's site has attracted settlement since the earliest times. As 'Velzna', this spot is believed to have contained one of the most important Etruscan cities before the Romans sacked it in 264 B.C. Now firmly on the international tourist trail, Orvieto is an economically and culturally thriving place with an extremely convivial atmosphere.

While everyone should visit the *duomo*, those undeterred by stairs should also climb the Torre del Moro ('Moor's Tower') on Corso Cavour for jaw-dropping views of the city and its surrounding landscape. Those without claustrophobia should consider the 'Orvieto Underground' tour of ancient subterranean passageways, while those not dieting should sample the impressive ice cream at Gelateria Pasqualetti in the Piazza del Duomo. But the best thing to do in Orvieto is simply to wander the labyrinthine network of medieval lanes – especially in the late-afternoon / early-evening hubbub, when exquisitely dressed Italians and delighted tourists are milling round happily chatting to each other, slipping in and out of stylish boutiques, and wondering which particular excellent restaurant they might eat in tonight.

Getting to Orvieto from Bolsena is a simple matter of driving into Piazza Matteotti and following the road that winds up and out of the town (Via G. Marconi, later becoming Via Orvietana). All relevant turnings necessary for Orvieto are clearly signposted. There'll be a turn to the left when you've climbed most of the way out of Bolsena's volcanic crater, and at some point on this short stretch before you make your next left turn, you'll be leaving Lazio and entering Umbria. Nothing points this out to you, but you might notice that the landscape suddenly becomes more self-consciously aesthetic. Even the trees strive to place themselves at more pleasing intervals...

Trip 2. Bagnaccio hot spring (16½ miles / 27 km)

Heated by the earth's core and bubbling out of the ground at the temperature of freshly-made tea, this spring set in fields outside Viterbo has been channelled into a series of shallow bathing pools – each with a different temperature. Soaking yourself in the sulphur- and calcium-rich water is *allegedly* good for respiratory and rheumatic complaints, but it is *certainly* deeply relaxing, and your skin feels fabulously soft for hours afterwards. The happy atmosphere of the place is good for the spirit, too. People from various European countries stroll around in their swimwear, sit in the water chatting, sipping drinks, even smoking cigarettes (unfortunately). It can feel like an amiable cocktail party which just happens to be taking place in a field in the middle of nowhere.

The site is called Bagnaccio (which roughly translates as 'nasty old bath'), but you won't have heard of it because no one makes any money from it and therefore no one advertises it. The Romans used to bathe here and the site has changed remarkably little in 2,000 years. Completely unregulated, there are no showers, no changing rooms, no entry charges, no cafés or kiosks, and no anti-slip surfacing round the edges of the pools. It really is just some vaguely egg-smelling hot water lying in the middle of farmland. Bagnaccio isn't the only outdoor hot spring for bathing near Viterbo, but it could be the most charming.

In warm months, sunset is perhaps the best time to visit, as the steadily cooling air makes a delicious contrast to the hot water. And the oranges and pinks of the sky cast exquisite reflections on the opaque turquoise liquid. Watching the moon rise and the stars come out while floating on your back in hot mineral water in the middle of an empty field is an unforgettable experience.

To reach the pools, head south from Bolsena along the Via Cassia, following signs to Viterbo. About 6 miles / 10km beyond

Montefiascone, take the turning to the right signposted 'Marta', 'Capodimonte', etc. Follow this road for a kilometre or two until you see a large chunk of an ancient building in a field on the left (it has some typical narrow Roman brickwork if you stop to look more closely). Turn left onto the little gravel road running in front of the ruin and follow it for another kilometre or more. You'll probably smell the sulphuric pools before you see them, but look out for parked cars and caravans or people sitting in the water. Park anywhere, and wander round in your bathing costume like everyone else.

Trip 3. Città di Bagnoregio (9 miles / 15 km)

Bagnoregio's Città surely presents one of the most arresting sights in central Italy. Even hardened italophiles are stunned by it – suddenly reminded what an exotic country this is, so casually capable of the extreme and the improbable. If those last two sentences are enough to get you to visit the place, do yourself a favour and don't read beyond the end of this paragraph. Enjoy the full, unforgettable surprise of confronting the thing free from pre-imaginings.

Still reading? (Don't trust me to guide you blindfolded?) All right, then. Bagnoregio's Città is visually the stuff of fairytales. Or at least the stuff of naff fantasy artwork. It's a primer of Medieval architecture perched on a plume of striped rock stranded in the middle of a Grand-Canyon-like landscape. All around, pale hillsides slowly collapse, their lower clay strata licked away by jealous streams. The only access is by a kilometre-long pedestrian bridge slung across a tree-lined abyss – its zigzag angles emphasizing the village's perilous, madcap location.

Twenty-eight centuries ago, Civitá was a large Etruscan town spread across an expansive outcrop of rock. Despite the rock regularly crumbling away at the edges, sending whole parts of town sliding into oblivion, plenty of Romans, medieval and Renaissance Italians were happy to carry on living and building in dwindling Civitá. To their terrible cost. At several places inside the village today you come across the single surviving wall of a house set on a sheer precipice, its window-holes and doorways framing nothing but blue sky. It's just a matter of time before the rest of the place tumbles out of existence.

Recent centuries saw the town firmly shifting its focus to what was once the nearby hamlet of Bagnoregio, sited on much sturdier ground. About 4,000 people are currently at home in Bagnoregio's tall buildings and solemn, straight streets, while Civitá's island of diminishing rock holds only a couple of dozen brave, year-round inhabitants. The few ginger-brown homes, however, are beautifully maintained and lavishly decked with flowers. Locals realize what an irresistible prospect their village presents to outsiders. The fact is, burgeoning tourism is saving Civitá. Its nickname might be 'la cittá che muore' ('the dying city'), but these days a steady trickle of visitors are bringing the place back to life, making it financially worthwhile for residents to stay put and giving extra urgency to engineers' attempts to prop the rock up. (No one's found a way to stop the rot yet, but they surely try harder with every euro spent in the tiny art studios and cafés.)

At only 9 miles from Bolsena, Bagnoregio's Civitá presents a very short trip to another world. To get there, turn to Ride 2 of the RECOMMENDED BIKE RIDES and follow the directions given in the two paragraphs beginning "From Piazza Matteotti..." (ignoring cyclocentric references to things like "protesting leg muscles", of course – unless you drive with unusual vigour). Depending on the time of year, you might be asked a small payment for parking at the 90° right turn. The car park lies at the foot of the pedestrian bridge. As Cività's 'face' points westward and is best illuminated by p.m. light, you might prefer to make your visit later in the day rather than earlier.

Having tottered in a state of exhilaration across the bridge, you'll face a sobering climb up its steep final slope and the stone steps that follow. (Generally I would say that Cività isn't *completely* inaccessible to anyone with impaired mobility, but you'll be meeting a stiff challenge on the slope and the long shallow steps. Wheelchair-users will need real determination and the help of a strong friend. The steps do include narrow ramp sections for the passage of wheels, but what use they'd be for wheelchairs is questionable. Once or twice I've seen determined young Italians nimbly going up and down them on mopeds.)

At the top of the steps, you'll pass a shattered building on the left before entering a tunnel-like city gate – part of the original Etruscan settlement, with a frontage added in the 13th Century. Strangely, all that remains of Cività today is the area constituting the central and most important part of the city (it's sort of like London falling to bits while Westminster stays standing). The street you come in on, Via Santa Maria, is part of the old *decumanus maximus* – the major east-west axis of grid-planned Etruscan and Roman settlements. It is still the main route through the village. After you emerge from the tunnel into a little piazza, look right to see a mono-walled building with window-holes gazing onto the void. Then carry on a few paces towards the main church (formerly a cathedral, until Cività shifted its focus to Bagnoregio) on Piazza San Donato. This square, once crossed by the ancient *cardo maximus* or major north-south axis, would have formed the civic and religious epicentre of the city for Etruscans and, later, Romans. Note the stubby remains of Roman columns in front of the church. Did they once mark the entrance to a pagan temple built on the same site?

Apart from nosing around some of the intriguing erosion-severed alleys running off to right and left, there's really nowhere else to head in Civita except along the *decumanus maximus* (which continues just to the right of the church) until it opens onto a spectacular view of collapsing hillsides. On the way to this view (or on the way back) you should consider investigating the *stunning* snacks and wine served in the cavernous building facing the southern flank of the church – all local produce. You should also look out for one or both of an elderly couple who often sit on the low wall outside their house further along the same street. If they invite you into their garden to see the 'panorama', for heaven's sake *go and see it*. (If they don't invite you, *ask* if you can see it.) Their garden has easily the best view in the whole village – and they've also assembled a weird, ramshackle little folk-museum of farming implements and whatnots from various centuries in little caves behind their house. Admire their enterprise, and be sure to give them a few coins when you leave.

Dedicated explorers might like to know that if you continue beyond the view at the end of the street and follow the curving route down alongside Civita's rock, you'll eventually come to a large straight tunnel with daylight at its end. Piercing the outcrop of rock and running the full subterranean width of Civita, this walkable passageway was originally the *dromos* of Etruscan Civita – an access corridor to its necropolis.

Trip 4. Pitigliano (19 miles / 30½ km)

Like Orvieto and Civita di Bagnoregio, Pitigliano is spectacularly set on a high upthrust of tufa. Peninsula-shaped, this chunk of volcanic rock juts out from an ocean of dark green foliage. While the geological position is striking, what makes Pitigliano extraordinary is the number of dwellings shoehorned onto the site. Seen from afar, it's a mad shantytown – but of tall homes well-built in camel-coloured stone. Sprouting from each other's flanks like mushrooms, they vie aggressively for the same space, the ambitious skyscrapers of a medieval metropolis. Their original construction is hardly imaginable. "Pitigliano was not built. The cliff grew it," writes one dumbfounded photographer on his webpage. Each home on the perimeter is rooted on a sheer precipice, a cliff wall dotted with Etruscan caves. It seems more a painting than a real view. The artist has intricately rendered the buildings, patiently repeating black rectangles for windows and dabbing jaunty red brushstrokes for terracotta roofs. The supporting mass of rock has been merely sketched, detail fading into stylized suggestion. The foliage far below is just a sponged-on wash of colour, spreading out beyond the margins of the picture.

While still very high in gasp-factor, the first view of Pitigliano presented to motorists travelling from Bolsena is perhaps not the most spectacular available. You should carry on beyond the town down a series of long hairpins, following the SS74 signposted for Manciano. After crossing a tall bridge and beginning to climb uphill, stop beside a prominent church on a sharp bend and gaze across the valley at the full breathtaking stretch of the town.

Inside, Pitigliano is a charming mix of imposing architecture and homey cobbled lanes. Wanderers in the shade of tall buildings meet sudden bright glimpses of plunging valley view. Some of these atmospheric alleyways were for several centuries home to a thriving Jewish community, and you might wish to seek out the old synagogue and associated buildings. Elsewhere in town you'll find a conspicuous basilica with a florid frontage and a wildly over-the-top altarpiece.

One thing you're unlikely to find in Pitigliano is a huge number of tourists. While the town isn't exactly unknown, visitor numbers are still small and, depending on when you go, you might feel you have the place pretty much to yourself. Indeed, the southernmost tip of Tuscany in which Pitigliano finds itself is unvisited generally. Far from the manicured, Italian-Cotswolds feel of central Tuscany, this area is wild, rugged, and startlingly empty. (If you find yourself charmed by the vast brooding landscape and have a penchant for views from high places, do also consider investigating the strange hilltop fort of Radicofani and the top-of-the-world summit of Monte Amiata, both an hour or so up the SS2 (Via Cassia) from Bolsena.)

To get to Pitigliano, head northwest out of Bolsena along the Via Cassia. After about 4 miles (6km), turn left at a bank of blue signposts onto the SS489, and carry on to Gradoli. Here you'll switch to the SS74, following signposts all the way to Pitigliano. Notice the muscular, empty terrain begins before you even cross the border into southern Tuscany.

Trip 5. Tarquinia (minimum 36 miles / 59 km)

Not many of us enjoy long car journeys, so I've restricted these recommended excursions to places less than 20 miles from Bolsena. But for Tarquinia, I had to make an exception. If you have any interest in antiquity, it is unmissable. And if you've caught the Etruscan bug, it is especially so. Elaborate paintings decorating the walls of Tarquinia's underground Etruscan necropolis offer the most detailed and vivid insights into Etruscan life available anywhere in the world. The town's wonderful museum, meanwhile, has one of Italy's best collections of Etruscan artefacts. In Tarquinia, perhaps more than anywhere else, the 'mysterious' and 'enigmatic' Etruscans finally take on flesh, step forward, and tell us about themselves.

Founded 3,000 years ago, around the time that Pharoanic Egypt began slipping into decline, this originally Villanovan settlement grew into one of the most powerful of Etruscan cities. At its height it housed 100,000 people inside a city wall 8 miles round, and its territory extended so far that Lake Bolsena was known as Lake Tarquinia. The city was concentrated on a large hillside, now empty save for farmers' crops and the very sketchy bases of buildings, gates, and gigantic temples. A parallel hillside, used by ancient Tarquinians for burying their dead, is currently the spot that holds all the excitement. Across this high plateau spreads a warren of 6,000 subterranean tomb-rooms – 200 of them decorated with wall paintings. The recovery of these burial chambers constitutes some of the world's first historical excavation work; some were unearthed as early as 1489. The majority, however, were brought to light in the 19th and 20th Centuries, and it's thought there are many still to be revealed. Only about a dozen frescoed rooms are open to the public at any one time – which sounds disappointing, I know, but the pictures are so revelatory that any more would surely boggle the mind (and leave insufficient time to visit the museum).

The paintings, the earliest examples of pictorial art in Italy, are lively and colourful – showing animated figures full of personality. There are scenes of hunting and fishing, of banqueting and ceremonies, of dancing and game-playing, even of sexual acts (some quite unorthodox). All were put there to remind the dead of what it was to be alive. In other tombs, mythical figures and fabulous beasts set a different tone. The oldest wall paintings date from the 7th or 8th Centuries B.C., and ideas on appropriate subject matter seem to have changed occasionally over the four centuries that followed.

When they weren't painting figures or animals, the Etruscan artists were busily surrounding their creations with bold patterns and little abstract designs. The effect, believe it or not, can be strikingly suburban – neat rooms adorned with dados, regency stripes, borders, chequerboards, polka dots, flowers, friezes, repeated shapes – and set you furiously wondering about the history of patterns and interiors. And while we're on intimations of modernity, look out for the boxer on the left wall of one of the tombs. His boots are absolutely indistinguishable in appearance from modern-day boxers' boots, and make 25 centuries suddenly seem like no time at all.

Fifteen minutes' walk from the necropolis site, the more modern town of Tarquinia is interesting in its own right. Partly walled, and dotted with medieval towers, it's set on an elevated spot commanding fine views down to the Mediterranean 3½ miles away. In the opposite direction, great hilly swathes of farmland roll off into the distance. Chief among the town's attractions is the Museo Nazionale Tarquiniese (National Museum of Tarquinia). A former palace, the Gothic-Renaissance building housing the museum includes a little central courtyard and offers stunning views from its uppermost floor (the strangely long, low steps that take you there were to allow horse-riders to move through the building!).

The ground floor is dominated by weighty stone sarcophagi topped with sculpted portraits of Etruscans reclining propped on one elbow (the traditional posture of guests at a banquet). On the upper floors, numerous rooms display: Villanovan artefacts; exotic objects indicating the Etruscans' contact with far-flung peoples; exquisite Etruscan gold jewellery, bronzes, painted ceramics and figures; two tomb-rooms with especially lively wall paintings transplanted here from the necropolis to prevent further decay; plus a hugely important collection of fine Greek pottery.

The museum's show-stopper, however, is the pair of terracotta winged horses saved from a local 3rd Century B.C. temple – the biggest Etruscan temple ever identified anywhere. Rendered with perfect realism, they bristle with impatience to trot onward. They were but a tiny detail on the original temple – what on earth must the rest of it have been like?

Lovers of Art Nouveau, by the way, should try to spot an astonishing Etruscan ceramic jug tucked away amongst dozens of other pots in a large display case. Its ribbed, pumpkin-like body and stylized organic neck and lip could easily have been the work of Lalique or Tiffany. Indeed it seems almost miraculous that this near-definitive example of a very distinctive design movement could have been fashioned in isolation more than 2,000 years before that movement occurred. The jug is dark grey and about a foot tall. You'll need a bit of luck to spot it amongst all the museum's other treasures, but you'll be in no doubt that it's the right one when you've found it.

Aware that most visitors come intending to see both, the museum and the necropolis offer a discounted joint entry ticket which it's worth buying at whichever of the two you visit first. Note that both places are open every day of the week *except Monday*. (Yes, there's bitterness in that italicization. My first trip to Tarquinia was on a Monday…) For current opening times, call the Tourist Information Office on 0766-856384.

There are several possible routes to Tarquinia from Bolsena. (**1.**) You can travel counter-clockwise round the lake, following the directions I give cyclists in Ride 1 of the RECOMMENDED BIKE RIDES but ignoring the very last "signposted left turn into Capodimonte" and carrying on to Marta, going on from there to Tuscania, and from there to Tarquinia. This route keeps you always on tiny picturesque roads and will tot up about 38 miles (61 km). (**2.**) Heading south instead down the Via Cassia (the only remotely 'major' or 'busy' roads in these parts), you can turn at Montefiascone towards Marta, thence to Tuscania and Tarquinia (totalling 36 miles / 59 km). (**3.**) You can stay on the Via Cassia, carry on past Montefiascone and turn off toward Tuscania shortly after entering the city limits of Viterbo (46 miles / 75 km).

(**4**.) Or you can follow the Via Cassia all the way through Viterbo (following signs to Roma), and head across to Tarquinia via Vetralla (46 miles / 75 km). This last option will take you past an aged stone aqueduct looping its way across hills outside Tarquinia. Except for Viterbo and Montefiascone, none of the towns mentioned in these routes is likely to slow you down much or catch you in an urban bottleneck. All turnings to the towns mentioned are well-signposted. Of course, you can always take one route out to Tarquinia and follow another back to Bolsena.

Hiring a car in Bolsena

At the time of writing, no one offers cars for hire in Bolsena. Car hire companies do operate in nearby Montefiascone, Orvieto, and Viterbo.

Taxis

Numbers in Bolsena include: 338-979-0846 / 0761-826852 / 347-211-7390 / 330-629629. If you're staying in a hotel, receptionists always have up-to-the-minute contacts and can do all the irksome booking in Italian for you.

Buses

It's possible to travel by bus to many towns around Bolsena, but timetables can be Byzantine. Often the only outward journey of the day is at the crack of dawn and the only return journey in the middle of the afternoon (this might suit some of you, of course). Just getting hold of bus schedules can be a struggle. At the time of writing, Bolsena's Tourist Information Office refuses to concern itself with things like bus schedules. The large green metal booth selling newspapers near the traffic lights by the mouth of Piazza Matteotti has some and helpful staff there will try to help you make sense of them.

Comments? Questions?
E-mail: fleurkinson@hotmail.com

INDEX

accommodation   40, 60–66
alphabet   16
amphitheatre   21–24
apartments – *see accommodation.*

Bagnaccio   87–88
Bagnoregio (also see Cività di
   Bagnoregio)   12, 59, 82–84, 88–
   91
bed and breakfasts – *see*
   accommodation.
bicycle hire   85
Bisentina Island   4, 11–12, 35–38,
   81
boat trips   4, 37–38, 39
buses   97–98

campsites – *see accommodation.*
Capodimonte   18, 81–82
car hire   97
cashpoints   70
castle (Rocca Monaldeschi della
   Cervara)   3, 13–14, 21–22, 34–
   35, 39
catacombs   4, 27–28, 33–34
chemist's   69
Church of Santa Cristina – *see Santa*
   Christina's Church.
Cività di Bagnoregio   59, 82–84,
   88–91
coffee   55–58
Colesanti, Nicola   39–40
Colosseum   22

coregone   51, 53
Corpus Christi / Corpus Domini
   29–32
Cristina – *see Santa Cristina.*

Dante   52
disabled visitors   63, 90
doctors   72

Egyptians   16, 18, 94
Elba, island of   6
emergencies   71–72
English newspapers – *see newspapers*
   in English.
Etruscans   3, 13–21, 36, 86, 89–96
Eucharist Miracle   29–33

Giglio, island of   6
Gradoli   12
Greeks   14, 16–18, 95
Grotte di Castro   5

hospitals   72
hot springs – *see Bagnaccio.*
hotels – *see accommodation.*

Infiorata   30–32
internet access   69
ice cream   54–55
islands on the lake – *see Bisentina*
   Island and Martana Island.

Lazio   3, 5, 16, 38, 86

101

NOTES

NOTES

NOTES